A catalogue record for this
work is available from the
National Library of Australia

Barter, David (author)
A Better Way
ISBN: 978-1-922527-84-4

Minion Pro 10.5/14

Book design by Green Hill Publishing

A BETTER WAY

A better way for life and ministry

DAVID BARTER

ACKNOWLEDGEMENTS

I would like to take a moment to thank a few people who have played a major part in my journey thus far.

Firstly, I would like to thank my amazing family - Emma, Ezekiel, Jack and Lucy. You have walked the pathway of recovery with me and have been a rock in my life. I am the most blessed man alive to have the privilege of marrying the most incredible woman in the world and to be the father of three amazing children. I couldn't think of a better life than the one I have with you.

I would also like to thank:

Ps Phil and Lyn Jagger, for being so open and embracing me in the darkest moments of my life. Thank you for being there and helping me in the early stages of my recovery. I will never forget the generosity and compassion you showed me.

Ps Andrew Gray, thank you for investing your time and wisdom. You have imparted so much and have had a tremendous impact on the person I am today. I have been so blessed to sit under your leadership and mentoring and I'm so grateful for everything you have done.

Ps Greg French, I am extremely thankful for your friendship and mentoring, you have walked with me through some of the darkest days. Your encouragement has been a constant stream of life for me. Thank you for believing in me and for encouraging me to write my story. This journey has been one of healing and transformation. You have been a gift from God to my family and to me.

Wendy Konemann, thank you for being such a great source of encouragement and wisdom throughout this book journey. I am so appreciative of the time and energy you have given to make this book a reality. Your knowledge and prophetic input has been timely and I am extremely grateful.

FORWARD

Our world is in constant change, growing in complexity and ever increasing pressure, stress, anxiety and depression, which is becoming far too common. In Australia, one in seven people will experience depression and one in four people will have anxiety in their lifetime.

In David Barter's book he shares his journey, the lessons learnt and gleaned. He also presents a preventative and corrective pathway forward. This book is both timely and important. My 35 years of pastoring and leadership has convinced me that emotional depletion is widespread and at almost epidemic proportions. If anyone is qualified to write a book on this topic, it's David Barter.

I know you will enjoy the ease of reading, and practical approach, in which David walks through each chapter of his very honest, personal journey. The book is also well researched and written with very practical guidelines. A wonderfully informative and helpful book,

Enjoy.

Greg French.
Mofn (Ment.H; Dev.D; Beh.p)

CONTENTS

1 Corinthians 12:27-31 The Message (MSG)

You are Christ's body—that's who you are! You must never forget this. Only as you accept your part of that body does your "part" mean anything. You're familiar with some of the parts that God has formed in his church, which is his "body": Apostles; Prophets; Teachers; Miracle Workers; Healers; Helpers; Organizers; those who pray in tongues. But it's obvious by now, isn't it, that Christ's church is a complete Body and not a gigantic, unidimensional Part? It's not all Apostle, not all Prophet, not all Miracle Worker, not all Healer, not all Prayer in Tongues, not all Interpreter of Tongues. And yet some of you keep competing for so-called "important" parts. **But now I want to lay out a far better way for you.**

INTRODUCTION

Welcome. This book is for those of us who are questioning if there is a better way to live life. It is a book for everyone containing principles God has taught me on my journey of being a pastor. My encouragement to you is to dive in and see how life can be different as we explore this better way. Throughout the book there will be areas that speak directly into a pastor's life. Take those principles and superimpose them into your context because the truths are God's universal truths.

I was right when I believed ministry could be done in a better way. I was in what some would say was 'a position of success and recognition,' implying I had made it to the top of the pile. And to be honest I thought I had. But even with all the "so called" success there was something deep within telling me there was a better way, that things could be and should be done differently. Little did I realise just how far God would lead me down the pathway of change. Breaking out of performance and an unhealthy desire for recognition has brought me to a place of contentment, which has made me a better person in every way.

God's ability to lead me on a pathway which is both truth filled and authentically real has been a journey for which I am humbly grateful. My words will never be able to express the depth of gratitude I have for what God has done for me.

I can truthfully say there is a peace within me regarding my identity and my purpose which I've never felt before. Although the future is not what I once thought it would be, I have come to a place in myself where I'm ok with that. I choose to rest in what God has put in my hands, loving the people He has trusted me to lead and shepherd.

I now live with a burden in my heart, to bare my soul to those who are thinking there must be a better way and are suffering in silence. There is a better way in which wholeness and contentment walk hand in hand.

CHAPTER ONE

The Why

Some might ask 'Why write this book at all?' And to be honest, I have asked myself the same question, "What do I have to say that we haven't heard before? Do I really have anything new to say that might help someone?" Well, for some, maybe I don't. I'm ok with that. Maybe this book isn't for you. But there are others who, like me, have been walking through the wilderness trying to figure out why things are the way they are. Why is ministry life so hard? Why do I keep falling into a dark hole?

If you find yourself asking these questions then I believe what I have to say will help you discover a new way, a way which will help you answer your deep longings on the inside. My heart is to help those who are desperate for things to change. If I can help just one person to find breakthrough, then I have achieved my goal.

———

To understand the reason for writing this book I need to share a little about my past and shine a light on who I am and what I've walked through.

I grew up in a single parent home. My dad left when I was five years old and my mum was left to raise myself and my two older brothers. Some years later mum married again and had another two boys, which made me one of five. Unfortunately, my mum's second marriage didn't end well, either. My stepfather was an alcoholic, and ultimately, due to his struggle with alcohol, their marriage became destructive for all of us. However, life was good with mum and she gave us everything she could, and I'm thankful for her. Unfortunately, my dad was distant through my childhood and up to this day we are not overly close. As a kid I would see him once or twice a year at best, but as I've grown older things have gotten a little better and we are in more regular contact, which is nice.

Growing up without a father definitely had a negative impact on my life. I remember living the rejection over and over again as I grew up. I realised at a young age the reality of my father not embracing me in his life and this damaged my soul, leaving me with a gaping void of brokenness and pain.

Early in my teen years I started to experience the beginnings of depression. I didn't know it at the time, but it would be the start of a twenty seven-year battle with mental illness which would include three emotional breakdowns and four years of medical treatment including medication and multiple sessions with a psychologist. The crazy part of it all was the fact that this continued to go on even after I gave my life to Jesus in 2002. I did two years of Bible college, then became a Youth Pastor. After this I was appointed as a Senior Pastor; and then spent almost five years as a Campus Pastor in one of Sydney's mega churches. All the time I was struggling with depression and anxiety.

I spent years ignoring my emotional condition. I refused to stop and take stock of my life, believing this struggle was the only way - it was my 'cross to bear'. The rare times I tried to deal with the depression and anxiety, I would push into the spiritual side of things and spend hours praying and rebuking the enemy, yet I would struggle on with no breakthrough or freedom. I was ignorant, completely clueless, about what was really going on and how to deal with it. I was broken on the inside and the wound ran deep within me. This wasn't just a spiritual issue. There was a whole lot of unresolved hurt and pain deep down which needed to be processed. It needed more than just an engagement in spiritual warfare for me to experience freedom. We must never forget that our emotional and spiritual healing walk hand in hand; God works in both. True inner healing comes when we are willing to engage God in both the spiritual and physical realms. Maybe this is the key for you as well.

———

I say all this because I want you to know the past is not something to escape. We will never forget our past. It has shaped us into the person we are today - the good, the bad and the ugly. God didn't hit the delete button on our past when we received salvation. God doesn't want us to forget our past, He wants us to come to terms with it and overcome it. He wants to redeem our past. Our new self needs to meet our old self and settle the account. This means we must learn to take stock of our lives and ask ourselves the hard questions about why we are the way we are. I have come to understand the importance of emotional health and how vital it is to longevity in ministry. As Peter Scazzero says in his book, *Emotionally Healthy Spirituality*, 'Emotional intelligence is an essential part of becoming spiritually mature.' Emotions are the language of our soul and we must listen to them and make the necessary adjustments for us to live a complete and full life.

THE BREAKDOWNS

A breakdown is defined as a loss of mental and/or physical health. It is a complete loss of ability to cope with life and its challenges.

————

A breakdown doesn't always look the same for everyone. In my experience of dealing with depression, most people wouldn't have realised just how bad I was. Depression isn't always the look of sadness. It doesn't always look like hurt and pain. It doesn't always look like loneliness and isolation. Depression more often than not carries the mask of happiness and the facade of wholeness. It is hidden by the words, 'I'm ok,' and is disguised behind a smile and humour.

————

As I reflect, I can remember three distinct moments over the last ten years when I experienced a breakdown. The first time it happened I just pushed it away and buried it as quickly as possible. I put on my 'big boy pants', as they say, and 'pulled my socks up'! It lasted about a day and I pushed it so far down internally it didn't raise its head again for a few years. This experience was a warning sign that I didn't acknowledge. I should have been listening, but I chose to ignore the signs which ultimately resulted in breakdown number two.

————

The second time I had a breakdown it was a lot worse. I couldn't control my emotions and it took on a life of its own. I remember it so clearly. One day I was fine and felt strong, and the next day I was not. The weeks leading up to my breakdown were some of the greatest times I had experienced in ministry. Our church was growing, people were getting saved nearly every week and we had launched a service in another town reaching out to those in need and isolation. The results of what God was doing were amazing to say the least. I felt like I was on top of the world. Then, just like that, it all changed.

Within days I went from feeling invincible to complete and utter despair and brokenness. One day I got in the car to go to the supermarket and on the way back I felt this overwhelming sadness and I started to cry uncontrollably. By the time I pulled into the driveway I was a mess and couldn't get out of the car. I just sat there crying but not knowing why. After an hour my wife came out and found me. She helped me get out of the car and into my bedroom and that's where I laid with the door shut, confused and scared about what was happening.

This was the scariest moment in my life. Everything was different and I couldn't control my thoughts, which raced through my mind and made me feel crazy. It was a frightening chaos in my head. I felt like I had lost the ability to think clearly and I had voices speaking to me calling me names and telling me to do all sorts of horrible things. There was no doubt the voices I was hearing were demonic in origin.

I was experiencing recurring panic attacks for days - they were so overwhelming I would curl up and cry uncontrollably. I couldn't eat or sleep. Interacting with others was so draining because I would spend the whole time just trying to hold it together and hope they didn't notice anything. I spent all my energy trying to hide what I was struggling with. At this point I still hadn't discovered the need to open up and let people in. I was afraid that if I did open up and share what was happening, then I would be seen as a failure, I would lose my job and everything I had achieved would have been for nothing.

After days of trying to survive what was happening, I finally did open up, and asked my wife to contact pastor friends of ours. After speaking to them on the phone, my wife put me in the car and drove me to their house. I was a complete mess when I arrived. I couldn't control my emotions and I was experiencing severe panic attacks. I sat with them for hours as they prayed with me and led me into the beginning of my recovery. I am so thankful for this couple. They were so kind and loving, and the way they ministered to me was exactly what I needed at the time. I truly don't know what I would have done if they weren't in my life. I am so aware of how fortunate I am to have people in my life I can turn to, and I feel deeply for those who are struggling, but feel they have nobody they can reach out to.

THE WAKE UP CALL

I had spent years denying the truth about what was going on with me, trying to deceive myself into believing that, just like the Apostle Paul, the depression and anxiety was my 'thorn to carry'. When we live with self-deception long enough we end up trying to normalise something that is not normal, we justify our experience as something God has given us to keep us humble. We tell ourselves things like: 'This is part of the deal of ministry, so just grin and bear it'; 'It's not about me anyway. Isn't it all about Jesus?'; 'My life doesn't matter anymore'; 'Do whatever it takes to win the lost'; 'It's all about growing the church'; 'Get more people, fill every seat'. Of course, there is truth in all of these statements and at first appearance they sound noble, but the reality is, none of those beliefs are sustainable if we are emotionally broken and hurting on the inside.

These were the fractured conversations I was having with myself regularly. I needed to wake up! I needed to snap out of it because it was killing me, I was burning myself out and I was broken. I was trying to make my struggles a spiritual achievement. The problem is though, there's nothing holy about self-neglect, and looking back I can see just how immature and foolish I was.

———

I remember a time when my eldest son Ezekiel was just born. My wife, Emma, would be woken up multiple times a night because my son would cry or need to be fed. It was crazy how many times she would get up at night for him. It definitely wasn't put in the fine print when we thought it would be a great idea to have a baby!

Night after night Emma would wake up whenever he cried, and so would I, to help her get him sorted. Waking up lasted for about a month for me and then I started to sleep through the crying. It got to the point where Emma could physically kick me and I still wouldn't wake up. The next morning she would be frustrated at me, and when I asked why she was upset she would say, "Couldn't you hear the baby last night? Didn't you feel me kick you?" My response was always, "No, I didn't hear a thing. Did he wake-up last night?". Ironically, I never learned from my experience. The same thing happened with my second eldest son, Jack. What made it more difficult with Jack was that he had severe reflux as a baby and this made it ten times worse for Emma. But there I was, sound asleep and ignorantly unaware of what was going on.

I think she believes to this day that I was lying, and to be honest, there were a handful of times I can remember hearing him cry. I would just pretend I was asleep and wait for Emma to get him sorted, but most of the time I honestly didn't hear anything. I think the reason why I stopped waking up was because I knew Emma would take care of it, so I got used to it not being my responsibility, and this gave me permission to ignore what was going on.

———

This is how it can be for us in life. Our emotions can be screaming at us trying to get our attention, trying to wake us up to listen and take action. Often we are too busy to stop and listen, so we just ignore what our emotions are telling us. The problem is, you are the only person who can wake you up. Nobody else can sort the problems you are facing. People can help you and point you in the right direction, but ultimately, you have to take responsibility to wake up.

———

The wake-up call came to me when I had my second breakdown. This experience was the hardest thing I have ever walked through. It was somewhere in the middle of all the turmoil of the breakdown that I made a decision to beat the depression, and that I would do whatever it took to find freedom. At the same time as I was struggling through my breakdown, my eldest son Ezekiel was also having a battle with night terrors and anxiety. He was 9 years old at the time and I had been trying to help him deal with the fear and worry he was experiencing. As I was helping him overcome his battle, I realised I was also speaking to myself, and I finally became aware I had a reason to fight.

My kids became the driving force behind me getting serious about overcoming what I had faced for so many years.

From that time on I started telling myself and God, "I will overcome this to show my kids that there is nothing in life we can't overcome when we have Jesus."

———

At some point in the journey, if we want to be free from what we are going through, we need to find the reason which will cause us to turn around and face the problem. We have to find our reason to fight, and then proclaim it every day until it is so ingrained in us that it becomes our mantra for victory.

MY TURNING POINT

Let me ask this question, "How many wake up calls do we need before we make a decision to take action and turn our lives in a different direction?" I have lost count of how many times I've realised the need for change, yet have not actively done anything to make the changes needed to turn the page on that chapter of my life. But thankfully as I get older it is getting easier to see the turning points coming, and I find myself more willing to embrace the opportunity to be intentional in making the hard decisions regarding my life. This hasn't come easily though. It is true what they say about learning from our mistakes. Most of life's lessons are learnt in the unfairness of life; when our lives are broken and full of pain. For some reason God takes advantage of these moments and uses them to produce something good.

———

So how do we identify turning points in our lives?

*   **Turning points come disguised as pain.**

Often we miss a turning point in our lives because it looks and feels like pain. The reason we miss it is because we are conditioned by past experiences to turn away from pain instead of turning into pain. Self-preservation tells us to flee from whatever threatens us. We also can live with the false belief that God wouldn't lead us into a place of pain and suffering, which is totally untrue. All through the Bible we see suffering as a part of the Christian experience. Actually, it was a key element to the most important turning point in human history - the death and resurrection of Jesus Christ. Without Jesus suffering, none of us would gain salvation and make it to heaven.

*   **Turning points come through the storms of life.**

I believe every storm is an opportunity for us. Storms can catch us off guard and have the appearance of being out of our control, which is true most of the time. When we realise that out-of-control storms are rarely the problem, but rather how we hold ourselves in the storm is what matters most, then we are able to see the opportunities before us even though things are chaotic. Jesus often has a habit of coming to us in the middle of the storm, when things are out of control and fear and panic are trying to apprehend our spirit. It was at this point in the disciples' experience in the boat that Jesus told Peter to come out on the water. The key to seeing the turning points in the storm is to locate Jesus.

*   **Turning points come with discomfort.**

One of the ways God will get us prepared for change is by getting us uncomfortable in our current situation. It's a little bit like when we put our shoes on and tie one shoe tighter than the other. As we start walking there is a feeling something is not right, there's a discomfort and it bothers us until we are willing to do something about it. Discomfort makes us ask questions of ourselves that we would not normally ask, and it is the asking of these questions that ultimately leads us to change.

*   **Turning points come with unanswered questions.**

More often than not, when a turning point presents itself in our path it will come with a lot of unknowns. We may know it is time to make some changes in our life but we aren't sure if the opportunity before us is the right move. The question we need to ask ourselves is, "Is the pain it would take to change more bearable than the pain I would experience to stay the same?" Life is full of unknown information, the best we can do is take the information we do have, bring it before God and seek His guidance, and then make a decision on the direction we will go.

———

It takes courage to embrace a turning point. Often people think strength is about sticking it out, and this can be true in some circumstances, but we need to be careful that the reason we are staying isn't because of the fear of change. Most people are not comfortable with change and will do their best to avoid it. We do this because we are looking for certainty. We want answers to all the 'what if's' in the process of making change happen.

I experienced this when I realised it was time to resign my last position of employment. I had felt in God it was time to move on, and my time at this employment was coming to an end. I needed to start thinking about my future. It wasn't a surprise God was speaking to me this way because I vividly remember a word God impressed on my heart ten years earlier when we first became senior pastors of the church. God had said there would come a time when He would ask us to leave the church - this placement was just a season, and He had something else for us. So, when I started feeling unsettled, I knew change was coming. The problem was I didn't have a clue what was next. There was no job offer. I had no clear direction at all. As the time was approaching to send my resignation letter, I was getting increasingly concerned about the decision I had made. I started to second guess myself and contemplated just sticking it out.

I started to come up with all different kinds of solutions I could present to my boss which would mean not resigning. Ultimately I knew it wasn't the role I was in which was the problem. This was God leading me to something new which was never going to be in my current situation. I remember writing my resignation letter, and when it came time to send it my finger hovered over the send button for what seemed like an eternity. It was a scary thing I was doing - actioning a decision without knowing what was next.

This was a matter of faith and trust for me. It was a 'rubber meets the road' experience which God used to test me in what I truly believed about Him. We can talk all we want to about our faith in God, but until it is tested, it is just talk. Don't ever think God won't test your faith; His testing is part of the process of maturing as a Christian. 'Will I trust God despite all the unknowns?' The answer to this question will lead us either into what God has for us, or away from it.

———

Faith will always challenge the very core of what we believe. It will confront our thinking and require our minds to be transformed to embrace the essence of what faith is. When faced with a turning point in life it will take all the faith we have to take the first step in the direction God is leading us. Often we pray for God to give us more faith, but this is the wrong request to ask of Him. God gave us faith when we came to Him through Christ; it took faith to turn to Christ. The Bible tells us that faith as small as a mustard seed can move a mountain, so it is not more faith we need, but rather we need to activate the faith we have. God has given us all that we need to follow Him, but it is up to us to flick on the switch of faith so we are living in the assurance it brings about our future, even if there are a lot of unanswered questions.

SAYING YES TO CHANGE

Change is one of those things we seldom want to face in our lives. Change makes us uncomfortable and uneasy. We are creatures of habit and most of our lives are built around a revolving series of behaviours which give us the illusion of security. But what happens when the patterns on which we live our lives fracture, when life becomes unbearable, and nothing aligns with how we think it should be or how it used to be? This is the ultimate reality of change, it will happen whether we like it or not and it's inevitable in all our lives.

If we refuse to change on our own accord then life will eventually force change upon us. Nothing ever stays the same. Whether we like it or not, we are different today than we were a year ago. We are constantly evolving as a person through life's experiences, good and bad. Life requires change to grow. To refuse change is a refusal to grow.

———

I can still recall the turning point which set me on the journey to discovering a better way of ministry, and ultimately a better life. I was at a pastor's Christmas party. This was something we attended yearly as a celebration of the year and all the great things which had taken place. These dinners always made me feel a little out of place, and I would always dread having to attend because it put me out of my comfort zone. I didn't feel like I could be myself because of the other people in the room who were very different from me. As I was interacting with the other guests throughout the night, my pastor was watching me from across the room. He was obviously noticing things about how I was interacting with people and the discomfort I was experiencing. At the end of the night he approached me and said he would like to catch up with me the following week. This wasn't abnormal as I would regularly meet with him and discuss where I was at with my mental health and how I was coping with life and the church, etc. When we met up the next week, he started to talk to me about what he observed at the party and he made one statement which opened my eyes to a turning point moment.

The statement was simply, "You don't fit here!" And he went on to explain why he thought this way.

At first the comment was a little off putting. It touched a part of me where rejection had lived since I was a child, and I could feel the pain bubbling inside me. After a few days the words settled in my thinking and I started to realise he had put words to something I was feeling, but didn't know how to articulate. See, deep down I knew I was a square peg trying to fit into a round hole. I was totally aware I didn't fit in my current environment. It wasn't news to me. I just had never been truly honest with myself, and thankfully, my pastor was.

The problem was, though, I had a deep need for acceptance and recognition in my life. I hadn't paid attention to the small voice telling me things needed to change. The conversation with my pastor was the moment I was able to agree with what the small voice was telling me. It was the beginning of taking the first step of turning a corner, which has changed my life for the better.

I had to learn to say yes to change - not something I was accustomed to - but definitely something I desperately needed in my life. I needed to change my perspective on what change really was. Instead of seeing it as a negative thing I started to see it as an opportunity, something that would turn out for good. Shifting my thinking around change has made it possible to embrace the 'better way journey' and I am so thankful my pastor had the courage to have the hard conversation with me, to challenge me to not settle for something less than what God has for me. That conversation empowered me to say 'yes' to change.

Maybe today you need to have someone challenge you to reconsider your current situation. Unless we are willing to accept there are things which are not right, then we will never be willing to start the process of change, and at the end of the day we will continue in the frustration and confusion which is tormenting us. Let me be the person to be bluntly honest with you. If you don't do something about your situation you will never experience the freedom God so desperately wants you to have in your life. It's time to say 'yes' to the change you know in your heart needs to take place, 'yes' to the better way God has for you.

CHAPTER TWO

The road to recovery

LEARNING TO LET GO

One of the hardest things in life can be letting go of something which you have invested so much into. I think as humans we hold on to things because we don't want to feel the sense of loss that comes with letting go. The sense of loss makes us feel uncomfortable, and letting go pushes us into an environment of change. What we need to understand, though, is that we can never take hold of the next thing until we are willing to let go of the last thing. When we are climbing a ladder we will never get to the top unless we are willing to let go of the rung we are on. The same is true in life. If we want to move forward then it's time to start letting go of what was, so we can grab onto what will be.

Things we may need to let go of:

*   **Letting go of the past**

One of the most difficult things to let go of in our lives is our past. And to be honest, we can never really forget the past. It will always be with us. What we can let go of is our identification with the past and the hold the past has had on us. Everyone has a past, whether it be good or bad. We cannot escape the reality that we have lived our lives and have had experiences, some of our own doing and others that were not our own. Some of us have had things happen which should never have happened, and it can be hard to reconcile these things with God, especially if what happened was out of our control and completely wrong. It is helpful to remember, when looking for answers in regards to these past experiences, that we don't live in a perfect world, we live in a fallen world which is full of sinful behaviour, yet God has never left us and is focused on redeeming our painful experiences. He wants to transform us and use those experiences to draw us closer to him and make us more like Jesus. It is the things which have taken place throughout the years which God has used to shape us into the person we are today.

I believe the best way we are able to let go of the past is to be thankful for it. Sometimes it isn't about being thankful for what happened because it was a completely despicable act, but rather being thankful for what God has done to deliver us and redeem us from the situation. We spend a lot of time living with a negative attitude in regards to the experiences we have gone through. We carry the shame, regret, failures and pain we have experienced and we allow them to define who we are. We let the mistakes determine the direction we will take in life and find little happiness because we are so focused on getting away from the pain.

But when we take the approach of finding the things we can be thankful for, and we start to thank God for all He is and has done in our lives, then we are truly able to let go and start to look to the future with an understanding that 'all things work for good for those who love God and are called according to his purpose'. The past was never meant to define us…but it definitely is meant to grow us as a person.

*   **Letting go of relationships.**

Relationships come and go in life. There are people we have with us for a short season, and then those who are with us for a long time. Relationships make up such an important part of our lives and have the power to make or break us as a person. Understanding the connections we have with others and why we are in a relationship with them is such a valuable thing. I believe without a doubt that some friendships have a sunset on them. The person is in our life for a season and for a purpose and when the purpose of the friendship is fulfilled, the sun will set and it's time to move on.

I have seen first-hand when a healthy relationship turns toxic, because people have tried to keep a connection alive, but God intended for it to end. This can happen a lot in church life, normally with people who are toxic. They take offence at someone or something in the church, and because of this offence they end up leaving the church, yet want to continue to stay in fellowship and connection with some of the members of the church. As time goes on, if these relationships are entertained, things become unhealthy because the connection was meant to be severed when the person left the church. As the connection continues it becomes destructive and almost always results in more people leaving the church.

Sadly, over the years I have seen marriages fall apart because of spouses reconnecting with past romantic relationships. These relationships had long passed, their expiry date and were never meant to reconnect, only that social media played its part. More often than not it ends in disastrous outcomes for families and affects those involved for many years as they work through the hurt and pain of separation and divorce. It has become so clear to me when witnessing these moments in people's lives, that the relationships were severed for a reason by God and He never intended for them to reconnect.

*   Letting go of unrealistic expectations

Unrealistic expectations are a cause of great frustration in our lives, especially in relationships. Probably the greatest example of this would be in marriage, because it's the collision of two lives coming together, trying to intertwine previous life experiences and ways of living. If our expectations are not realistic in our marriage then there will be a lot of tension and arguments, which will lead us to live with resentment and frustration in our hearts. If we allow this to continue, ultimately the relationship can end in divorce and can damage our entire family.

When it comes to ministry, unrealistic expectations can cause deep frustration and lead us to disconnect from relationships. When we feel like someone has let us down because they never met the expectations we had of them, this can lead us to avoid them and write them off in our lives. The sad thing is, that a lot of the time in this type of experience, we failed to clearly communicate the expectation to the person and they are completely unaware they have done anything wrong.

We have to let go of our unrealistic expectations of people. Learning to accept that people will more often than not get it wrong, or will do something in a different way than we would have done it ourselves, will help us live our lives with less frustration. One thing I have learnt over the years of ministry is to accept and be ok with some frustration. When people are being empowered and released into the calling for their lives, they won't always get it totally right and frustration is to be expected. Frustration will always exist when we are working to develop people and is a normal part of the ministry God has for us. When we lower the bar for people in our lives and have realistic expectations of them, we also at the same time lower our own stress levels.

I have realised that if I lower my expectations of people to a more acceptable level, everyone is happier. Three things I try to remind myself when it comes to my expectations of people are:

1. I never expect people to do something I am unwilling to do myself.
2. I never expect people to do something the exact same way I would do it.
3. I never expect people to do something without communicating it to them first.

I don't always get it right, but I try to do my best in empowering people and setting them up for a win by giving them realistic expectations. I allow them to achieve the outcome by supporting them and encouraging them, even if it takes longer and is done differently. This approach has dramatically lowered my stress levels in ministry and has created a healthier environment for my team to grow and learn.

*   **Letting go of hurt and pain.**

Ministry is a unique environment due to the immense amount of time we spend with people. Most of our ministry life is spent involved in peoples' lives, helping them with their problems and issues, helping them get unstuck and moving forward in their faith. Given the amount of time invested in people we can easily form bonds in relationships with people which go deeper than the normal employee/employer relationship, especially because the main call of a pastor is to shepherd people. Our role requires us to love and care for those God has put under our care. Given this reality it's not unusual for us as pastors to carry deep wounds within our hearts. Often you find that there are layers of hurt and pain from multiple people, in multiple locations over a long period of time, and unaddressed and unresolved wounds can feel like a death from a thousand cuts.

Betrayal, rejection and manipulation are the big three. If you have been in ministry for an extended period of time you would have most likely experienced one or more of these three multiple times, and if you haven't, just wait for it, it won't be long - it's on the way.

My greatest experience with the big three came eight years ago when I was pastoring my first church. We were inexperienced as pastors when Emma and I started leading the church. And because of our lack of experience we needed support from our board to run the administration of the church. There was one couple in particular who were very engaged and invested in helping us get on our feet and supported us through the first couple of years, which was a real God-send, and we felt blessed to have them alongside us. It was all working really well until I started growing in my leadership ability and was able to take on more of the weight of church responsibility. This led me to start making more decisions, and instead of asking the board permission to do things, I started leading and directing the board with regard to what we needed to get done and where the church was starting to head.

This shift in the power of the church was the trigger for this couple to start pushing back against my leadership. They started drilling down with control in the areas they held responsibility for. Things got so bad that eventually I had to request the husband's resignation from the board due to the lack of respect and level of control he was exerting over the board and the finances in the church.

This experience took a massive toll on me. The feeling of betrayal and rejection I experienced cut deep. This was when I had my first breakdown. I had never encountered this kind of situation before and really didn't know how to process what had happened. I carried the hurt and pain for many years after. What made it even more difficult was that I was still pastoring this couple. To cope with the negative emotions I would experience around them I had to learn to separate the behaviour from the person and trust God to do what only He could do, change their hearts. The only reason I allowed them to remain in the church was because I had felt a strong direction that God wanted me to. He had a deeper work to perform in this couple and part of the process was for them to have to remain in this situation. The amazing thing was that after a couple of years God spoke to the husband and he came to me and apologised for his behaviour.

So how do we deal with the hurt and pain we experience when in ministry? What can we do to safeguard our hearts so we minimise the damage? Below are some of the things I learned when dealing with the big three and the situation we were in. Embracing these principles led me to grow in my ability to deal with conflict and to learn to trust God with the process of change.

1. **Be kind to yourself.**

   Give yourself time to heal. Don't think you have to be some kind of superhero pastor. We are all human and we must accept that we have been hurt and that it will take time to process and heal from the experience. Often we can feel that if we are a good pastor then we are not allowed to carry hurt. This is not possible to achieve as our emotions are part of our makeup and cannot be pushed aside without dire consequences to our mental health. We have to give ourselves permission to heal in a way that pleases God.

2. **Learn forgiveness.**

Learning to forgive is the hallmark of being a Christian. When we choose to hold onto an offense it is like drinking poison and waiting for someone else to die. Forgiveness brings a release spiritually and physically. It's not always easy to forgive and sometimes it can take a continued approach of forgiving and repenting to find the final breakthrough. Forgiveness must be lived out and we have to be willing to walk the journey until we see the final breakthrough. The journey can be like a rollercoaster with many ups and downs in our feelings towards the person but, as we continue to bring it to God and release forgiveness we will eventually feel a release and know we have the breakthrough. So how do we know we have truly forgiven the person? When we no longer feel the angst deep in our chest when we see them, then we know the breakthrough has come and we have freedom.

3. **Repent if needed.**

Always stop and reflect on your own heart when going through this process, often there are things we will need to bring before God and repent of to be able to move forward. It could be as simple as an attitude which has been sitting under the surface and has been feeding the frustration and keeping the offense alive. Don't ever be afraid to admit offense and sin to God. This should be a normal part of our relationship with God.

4. **Talk to God.**

This is so important to remember, don't forget to speak to God about the situation. Ask Him to help you forgive and let it go. Ask Him to heal any wounds and to search your heart for anything that needs to be dealt with to be able to move forward in a healthy way. Talking with God is like sitting and talking with a good father. He will always listen and get involved because that's what a good father does.

5. Seek wisdom.

Finding someone you trust and speaking to them about what has happened and how it has made you feel will help you process what's going on. Getting wisdom on how to deal with the hurt and pain helps us make good decisions. Often if we are left to our own devices, we will make things worse because we are reacting from a wounded place in our hearts.

6. Excavate your soul.

This is a term my pastor, Andrew Gray, has spoken on many times. Learn to dig deeper into your soul. Reflect upon the situation and ask yourself the hard questions about why you feel the way you feel. What is beneath the hurt and pain? This is where real emotional intelligence is developed. Over time, as we learn to dig deep, we become experts in our own soul and learn how to navigate future issues. This is a journey of discovery and will lead us to great healing if we are willing to engage the process and be truly honest with ourselves.

7. Guard your heart.

We need to become experts at guarding our hearts. The Bible tells us to guard our hearts because the heart is the place where life flows from. A wounded heart cannot function in a healthy way unless it is healed first. This is not always an easy thing to do, but if we want to remain in ministry for the long haul, then we need to get serious about working on learning how to become experts in this area.

DISCOVERING REST

Everyone needs to learn to rest! Rest is essential when it comes to longevity in ministry. When pastoring my first church I was consumed with working hard and seeing results. I spent years pushing forward and not taking holidays. In the early years of leading the church I had a board who would express concern around me having too much time off because they were worried about the attendance and tithes dropping. To be fair, it was a reality whenever I went on holidays. I remember that by the time we transitioned the church as a campus of a much larger church, I had accumulated 12 weeks of annual leave. I hadn't had a proper holiday in years. This continued for another three years until I had my second breakdown. At this time my pastor told me I needed to have some time off and rest. Rest was such a foreign concept to me but I was in such a bad state that I could feel the need to stop for a few weeks, and I found it impossible to argue with him. This was the first time I realised how important rest is for sustainability in life.

A greater understanding came at the end of my employment in my previous church. After resigning my position and finishing up I took a six week break between jobs. For the first two weeks of my break I slept 14 hours a day, I felt so exhausted and worn out. I didn't realise just how much of a toll an unhealthy approach to rest had taken on me.

If there is one thing I could shout from the rooftop, it would be to get comfortable with having times of rest. Learn to stop and put your feet up. I wish someone had told me this years ago. Instead, I had to learn the hard way, and it cost me greatly in so many areas of my life.

I'm a different person today. I've made a commitment to myself to stop when I need rest and I will have days when I do nothing. At first when I started putting this into action I would feel guilty because I wasn't doing anything productive, but I have finally reached a place in myself where I have learned to love the art of 'nothingness.'

THE ART OF NOTHINGNESS

Doing nothing can sound easy at first thought, but when we put it into practise - well, that is a different kettle of fish! Believe it or not, there is an art to doing nothing, and it takes a lot of self-discipline to let ourselves stop and not do anything. I'm not talking about being lazy and slothing around being completely unproductive in life. I believe in working hard. What I'm talking about is having an ability to know when to stop and rest and also the strength to actually do it.

I find it interesting that as I am writing this part of the book we are all currently in isolation due to the Covid-19 virus. Right now, there are literally millions of people who have been told to stop and do nothing. We are all stuck in an extended, forced break. Yes, we have things we need to do, but generally we have more time on our hands now than we have had in years. Many of us are scratching our heads wondering what we can do to fill the days. This can be hard for someone who is always on the go and fills their life with all sorts of busy activities. To be honest, most of us are likely to be a little edgy and hanging for the moment we can get back to our lives! But what if, in all this craziness happening in our worlds, God is up to something? What if He is trying to show us a better way forward which will lead us into a more fulfilling life? It is possible that God is leveraging the current situation to teach us how to truly rest and to learn how to get comfortable with the art of doing nothing.

It would be a wasted opportunity for us to miss what God is trying to show us. If all we do as we come out of this season is return to the way things used to be, then we may have missed the point of what we have journeyed through. This is the greatest opportunity to re-evaluate our way of life and make the adjustments to live a more balanced, healthy existence.

I believe with all my heart that we all need to learn the 'art of nothingness' and include it into the fabric of our lives. We need to get comfortable with having times of doing absolutely nothing, and know we are allowed to, without feeling the slightest bit of guilt.

My wife, Emma, has been learning this lesson as well. Emma is a hard worker and is very dedicated to all that she puts her hand to. I am often amazed at her ability to juggle so many different roles in her life and how well she manages all of them. There are not many people I know who can be a professional teacher, business owner, pastor of a church, mother of three kids, be a dedicated wife, and still have all their marbles at the end of the day! As I have had to discover the art of nothingness in my life, I also have been sharing with her the need to learn to stop and do nothing. I had noticed how busy she was and how she wouldn't stop. Emma always had something she had to do or get done. The greatest blessing for her was when our daughter started school and we both found ourselves kid free for the first time in 14 years. I remember talking to her about the busy life she has and how she needs to learn to stop and rest, that even though some things seem important, they can wait if needed.

As I started to share with Emma what I had been writing in this chapter I could see the cogs turning and she was really listening to me. Something must have hit a chord with her because it wasn't long until there came a day where she sat and binge-watched her favourite Netflix show. We both find ourselves doing nothing most Mondays. This has been the biggest blessing to us both, and something which has helped recharge our souls.

———

THE ROAD TO RECOVERY

Recovery has been a long process for me, and to be honest, I am still walking its path. It's taken a lot of hard work getting to where I am today, and it has cost me a lot personally. Recovery will not happen for us unless we are willing to face the pain of the past and be willing to embrace the pathway ahead.

Some may say, "What do you have to complain about? You had it easy and others would have jumped at the opportunities you had!" They may be right, but one thing I've discovered on my road of recovery is that everyone has different capacities. What one person finds easy, another person will struggle with. It's very hard to judge another person's experience if we haven't walked in their shoes. We should treat people gently and with love and compassion, because we will never know when we may need it in return.

Recovery time is essential to having longevity in life and ministry. Athletes understand the importance of allowing their bodies to have the right amount of time to recover. Burnout happens because we don't allow ourselves to recover properly. Sometimes we are completely unaware of our need for recovery. We are not designed to run non-stop. The very fact that God created sleep for us tells me we are meant to stop and rest so our body and mind can recover from the day's activities and work. God Himself rested on the seventh day.

Allowing recovery time for ourselves is part of the process of the journey. Our spirit and soul need time to release the spiritual and emotional lactic acid which has built up due to times of high energy output. To successfully begin the next part of the journey we need to make sure we make an allowance for rest and recovery.

FINDING RECREATION

A big part of learning to rest and allowing myself to recover was to find recreation in my life. Recreation is an activity done for enjoyment when we are not working. When we find something we love to do, and make it a part of our lives, we are better for it. I had to give myself permission to have fun and enjoy life again.

My problem was I didn't really know what I liked to do in my down time. When asked what my hobbies were, or what I did for fun, I would default to one of two things: I would talk about my family and how I love spending time with my kids, or I would talk about how I love movies. Both statements are true, but they became a cover to a question I had no idea how to answer. To be honest, I didn't have an answer to the question. Depression had robbed me since I was a teenager of having any real joy in my life and I spent most of my time trying to avoid the daily battle it presented. This left little room to discover any kind or recreational enjoyment.

This was my life for years until just recently. Over the last two years things have started to change. The biggest key to the change has been the leadership and mentoring of my new pastor. I now regularly sit with him in mentoring sessions and we talk through life and ministry. One of his big things is emotional health and the importance of having a balanced life in and out of ministry. One day he asked me the question - the one I would always try and avoid or give the default answer to. That's right. You know what's coming! 'What do you do for downtime and for fun?' I knew the default answer wasn't going to work this time. My pastor is way too discerning and would not accept my avoidance to his question. He was looking for something more real. This conversation made me come face to face with the truth about my life. In that moment I realised just how much I had allowed myself to give up. I replied, 'I don't have any recreational activities!' For the next half hour all he spoke to me about was the importance of discovering what I enjoy. He challenged me to have new experiences, and I walked out of the meeting excited about what this could look like.

This was such a huge wake up moment for me which has changed my life. Since this conversation I have been on a journey of experiences. I have discovered I love working with timber and enjoy giving new life to old things. So I started a new hobby - restoring furniture in my spare time. I love doing it so much we decided to turn it into a business which restores vintage furniture, amongst other things. Now I get to take old, broken, worn-out furniture and give them a new lease on life. I get so excited when we deliver a piece of furniture to a customer and see the look on their face as they realise the transformation before their eyes. There's nothing like knowing you have made someone's dream come to life, especially if the furniture has come from a family member who has passed away. What we have done with the piece becomes a constant fond memory for the client of the one they loved, and the best part is the enjoyment I get from the process of transforming what's before me.

———

Our soul needs this type of outlet. Emotionally we need to be replenished by the things we love to do. When we constantly only do what we have to do, we end up living a joyless life full of obligation.

Ask yourself these questions:

- What do I love to do in my down time?
- What replenishes my soul?
- What needs to happen to start doing something I love?

———

If you can't answer these questions, then you have identified the need for change and it's time to get serious about finding a recreational outlet which will bring health to your soul. I suggest you start thinking right now about the three questions I've just asked. Grab a pen and write on this page the answers you come up with and then get to it and put your desire into action today!

CHAPTER THREE

Hitting the reset button

It wasn't a matter of continuing on in the current situation for me. I had reached a point where there was nothing to do but start afresh. I needed a new start, and the only way to do it was to hit the reset button on my life. This is the beauty of having a relationship with Jesus. He is not the God of a second chance but rather the God of another chance. When we have Christ in our lives, we are able to hit the reset button and start again. Realising our lives need a fresh start is the beginning of transformation, and the starting point is making a decision on the inside to start over.

Unfortunately, unlike a computer when we hit the reset button, we are unable to restore factory settings. We have to find a way to resolve the things in our lives which have shaped us as a person, and this is where God plays His part. He will take those experiences, good and bad, and use them to instil wisdom.

So, what does it look like to hit the reset button? How do we see the change we are desiring? I have walked this journey now for a few years and along the way I have learnt some lessons which may help us to start the process of starting fresh in life. It will take us being truly honest with ourselves, and with God, and we will need a willingness to engage our own heart to allow God to surface what He wants to show us.

This chapter is all about looking internally and really bringing the hidden areas of our heart to the surface. As you read, ask God to walk the journey with you. Don't rush through. It will take time to really be honest and dig deep to raise the truth to the surface, but it will be well worth the effort. The best way to do this is to take pen and paper and write down what God reveals as you start asking yourself the questions I have listed.

MEETING MY HUMAN SELF

Have you ever met yourself? You might think this is a weird question to ask. It's not like we can just run into ourselves at the local shopping centre, or go onto 'meet yourself.com'! But let's play with this idea for a minute. Let me ask you this question, "Have you ever met the person in the mirror?"

When my daughter Lucy was just a toddler, I would play a game with her called 'hello myself.' The way we played was to go into her bedroom and look into the mirror together and as we looked at our own reflection, I would ask her if she had met the girl in the mirror. She would look at me with a smirk on her face and a confused look which said, "My dad's a crackpot!" I would then go on to introduce her to herself and she would say, "Hello myself, nice to meet you!" We would play this game every time we went into her room and both of us would laugh at how weird it was to talk to our reflections.

It's funny how God can use a silly game like this to speak to us. God has shown me that part of the problem in my life was the fact I had never really met myself. I had lived my life trying to be someone, but I didn't know who that someone was. This is something I have grappled with for many years, and every day God is constantly revealing to me something new about who I am. Discovering who I am has become an exciting journey to walk, and I have been surprised more than once at what I have discovered. For instance, I have discovered I love my own company. I have never been someone who had spent time by myself. I had spent my entire adult life surrounding myself with people. I was always trying to distract myself from the depression and the thought-life that came with it. I was scared to be on my own. When we live in fear of our own thoughts, it's easier to fill our lives and keep busy to avoid facing those thoughts. When we are constantly running away and don't know how to stop, over time we become exhausted. There is no rest and we are unable to recharge our soul.

Knowing who we are is such an important part of learning how to rest. When we discover our identity in Christ we are able to become comfortable with who we are not. This is an extremely significant moment which brings us much freedom and leads us to contentment.

THE GIFT OF SELF REFLECTION

One of the greatest abilities God has given us is the ability to reflect, to be able to look at our lives and ask ourselves the hard questions about who we are and what we are doing. This ability is a key part of counselling and psychology today and is crucial to living a healthy and whole life.

This by far has been one of the most powerful tools I was given from my psychologist and is something I use daily. Reflection helps ground us when we are in turmoil. It forces us to stop and consider what is happening in and around us in real time. Reflection is one of the best learning moments we will experience in life, looking back on what has happened and allowing those things to educate us for the future.

Sadly, there are a lot of people who have never been taught how to reflect. Even if they have, they've never been shown how to find closure and healing from their past, so all that happens is a reliving of the pain.

Reflecting on our lives and what's in our hearts can be a confronting process, it can be hard to accept what we may find out about ourselves, but thankfully we are not alone in this process. God is the master inspector and He is willing and able to help us work through whatever is lurking in the untouched corners of our hearts. We must remember though, we are in partnership with God, and He can only help us deal with the things we are willing to acknowledge and confront.

The key to reflection is being willing to ask ourselves, and God, the right questions. David shows us this when he asks God to search his heart, to bring to the surface the things he needs to address and help him to move forward.

> *Psalm 139:23-24 (NIV)*
> *23 Search me, God, and know my heart; test me and know my anxious thoughts.*
> *24 See if there is any offensive way in me, and lead me in the way everlasting.*

Being willing to allow God access to your heart, and also being honest with ourselves, is such an important skill to develop in our lives. Below are some questions to help you start the process of reflecting on your internal world. As you ask yourself each question, bring it before God and let Him speak to you; you will be surprised with what He has to say.

> What am I feeling?
> Why am I feeling it?
> What is the truth in this situation?
> What is God saying about this situation?
> Do I need to repent, forgive or do both?
> What can I do to bring change?
> Do I need help to move forward or can I work through it alone?

I have found it takes courage to ask these questions of ourselves; to take an honest, real look at the internal life, and be open to whatever comes to the surface, willing to do what is needed to bring a course correction.

———

EMBRACING CORRECTION

Correction can be hard, but it is necessary if we want to start a 'better way journey.' Once we learn to reflect and identify the areas in our lives which need correction, then it's about implementing the changes needed. There are a few ways correction can come into our lives which we will discuss below, but regardless of how it comes there is one thing needed for it to affect change, and that is the ability to be honest with ourselves and our need for change. The first step is repentance for heading away from God and what He has intended for our life. Only then can we bring correction to our behaviour.

Ways in which correction comes:

1. Self-imposed correction.

All of us would do well to learn the ability to reflect upon ourselves and bring correction to the areas that need attention. Our behaviours, attitudes and thought life all need to be put under scrutiny. When we notice something isn't right we should ask ourselves the question, 'Why?' Understanding why we are feeling or acting a certain way empowers us to bring the correction needed to see the behaviour change in a positive way. Learning to self-correct can save us a lot of difficult conversations and even embarrassment. There is value in being self-aware and having a willingness to deal with the things you find out about yourself as you reflect.

2. Externally imposed correction.

External correction is good for us as well. Others can see things about us that we may not be able or willing to see ourselves, and their observations can be extremely helpful in helping us to avoid making further mistakes in life. They can direct us on to the right track so we are able to move forward. This is why having a mentor is such an enormous blessing and is so needed in ministry. I have devoted a whole chapter to this topic which will delve deeper into mentoring and the benefits it has for us.

Some of the greatest changes which I have made in my life have come from someone I trust seeing something in my life and bringing their observations to me. This then has led me to correct the problem before it became a major issue. I value constructive input like gold.

3. God's correction.

The Bible is clear that God will bring correction when He feels we need it. God is not scared to bring discipline into our lives which will lead us to repentance. Even though His discipline is not pleasant for us, He knows the end result will bring righteousness into our lives. When we allow God to correct us, we are displaying wisdom. A wise person will allow correction because they understand the value of discipline and how it impacts success in life. Nobody enjoys being disciplined. It can be uncomfortable and embarrassing, but when we understand and view God as our loving father, then we are able to receive it knowing God disciplines those He loves. All children who have appropriate boundaries and fair discipline in their lives end up being far better, well-rounded adults who respect authority and understand the value of correction. I am personally thankful for the times God has pulled me up and confronted an attitude or behaviour which, if left unchecked, would lead to bigger issues.

MAKING COURSE ADJUSTMENT

There are things in our lives that may not need correction, but rather an adjustment. We are on the right track but leaning a little too far to the left or right, and we just need to take a small step back into the middle of our own lane. If we allow the problem to go on too long, we will eventually end up completely off course and there will be a need for correction. If we get to it early enough, though, then a small adjustment will keep us on track.

I've experienced this on a number of occasions, normally in my attitudes toward things or people. This is the beauty of developing an ability to internally reflect upon ourselves. I remember a time years ago, being at church and greeting people at the door as they arrived. As people were coming in I was drawn into a conversation with someone and completely ignored one of the leaders as they came through the door. It wasn't intentional, but after it happened I became aware of how rude it must have seemed to the person. This played on my mind for the next 10 minutes and then the worship started, and I was standing at the front of the church worshipping and preparing myself to preach. I felt God put His finger on the issue and prompted me to apologise right there and then. Instantly I knew I needed to make this adjustment and do what God was leading me to do. So I walked over to the person in the middle of worship and apologised for being so rude when she walked into church. The funniest thing was, as I was speaking to her she just looked at me with a confused look on her face wondering why I was apologising. When I finished speaking she said to me, 'I'm not sure why you are apologising to me. I didn't even realise anything happened at the door when I walked in.' This is just one example of God teaching me how to make adjustments in my own heart so I stay on track.

Learning to listen to these little voices and inclinations on the inside has saved me from seeing problems grow, and become bigger than Ben-Hur. I really believe that God gives us little nudges from time to time so we have the opportunity to fix a problem before it gets out of control. The key is to become sensitive to God's leading and develop ears that can hear and eyes that can see the adjustments needed.

LEARNING A NEW WAY

I've discovered over the last few years that learning to do things a new way requires me to be willing to let go of things I thought were the right way, but were not. When we work within certain environments, we naturally align our behaviour to the culture and values we are exposed to. Our behaviour conforms to what is required, and we become focused on producing the results expected of our role. I have personally experienced this kind of thing in the past roles I have had. But what happens when you realise that the culture you are immersed in does not align with the values you have in regards to life and ministry? It's not always a right and wrong issue. Sometimes the problem is an internal, unsettled feeling that is telling us that what we are doing is not right for us and is not in agreement with who we are as a person. I've always tried to interact with people in a way which allows me to be able to go home and sleep at night. It's important to be able to live with our decisions and how we deal with situations as they arise. I have lost many nights of sleep because I have done something the way someone else would have done it, and then felt like a fraud because I knew, deep down, I wasn't being myself.

When we are exposed to an environment and culture which has strong patterns of behaviour in how they deal with people and issues, it's easy to get lost in it all. We can then just mechanically operate, going through the motions as the environment and culture dictates. The problem arises when we realise that our behaviours are in conflict with who we really are. When we become aware of this there is then a need for self-imposed re-education. We need to unlearn bad, negative patterns of behaviour and learn new ways of dealing with issues and people.

I've been going through a process of learning new ways of being a better pastor to the people God has put under my care. The more I read the Bible and books on leadership and ministry, I am seeing that God has a high expectation on us as pastors to not just lead people, but to care for them.

I have always had a heart to help people, no matter who they are, or where they are from. My experience after years of ministry working in different environments and cultures, is that we can pick up certain unhealthy behaviours and traits along the way. And it's these behaviours and cultural traits that need to be re-educated to align with the word of God and how He wants us to minister to His people. Don't get me wrong, No church or organisation is perfect. We all have good and bad traits in our environments and cultures, but relying on these norms is not an excuse when we stand before God. It's our responsibility to continually reflect on what we consider normal and make sure it aligns with the word of God.

We should always be working towards becoming better at who we are and what we do, and to be willing to allow the growth process to develop in our lives. An unteachable person is someone who is foolish of heart, and arrogance is their deception. As soon as we think we know it all, it's at this point we stop growing. There is no in-between when it comes to having a learning heart. We are either growing or we are not.

This being said, it poses the question, 'What about you? Are you ready to learn a new way?'

Steps to starting the journey:

- Expose yourself to new environments which will give you contrast.
- Look for new materials and resources that can show you a better way.
- Build relationships with those who are producing the fruit you are looking for.
- Find a mentor who will tell you what you need to hear, not what you want to hear.
- Be ruthless in uprooting unhealthy behaviours, attitudes and motives in your own life.

- Continually bring it all before God and allow Him to show you the way forward.

———

STRIPPING PERFORMANCE OUT OF RELATIONSHIPS

From the time I started in ministry there was a real culture of performance and comparison in the church environments I was connected to; not that this is the experience in every church, but it's definitely a trend in a lot of church environments. I started out as a youth pastor and the culture in the circles I connected with at the time was, 'the bigger the better'. All the talk was about how to get more numbers, how to grow bigger. It doesn't appear that much has changed since then. If anything, I can see it becoming more ingrained, and my concern is it's filtering into the next generation of pastors who are just getting started. In many places it is so deeply ingrained in the identity of how ministry is done that it can be seen in how people relate with each other, choosing only to connect with those in the room whom we think are a big deal, and promoting those who have the biggest statistics and are growing the fastest. The underlying desire in this goal is the unhealthy need to be recognised and paraded in front of our peers as one of the elite. This drives us to work harder, do more and push our people to achieve goals at all costs. It's a very sad reality in a large majority of churches today; too many good pastors are getting lost in the comparison trap and it's killing them, and the people God has entrusted them with.

How do I know this is what's happening? Because I'm describing myself. From the time I said 'yes' to ministry, I quickly learned from observing those around me that if I wanted to be 'someone in the kingdom' then I'd better be able to produce the results. This only became more ingrained as I progressed through the years and became more and more focused on achieving success and recognition.

When the ministry of the church starts to centre around numbers, it becomes easy to lose focus on what really matters. Meetings and discussions start to become more about crunching the service numbers. Attendance, money, visitors, salvation, rededications, baptisms, and small groups....The list can go on and on. Meeting for hours, pouring through reports, and all the while comparing your own results with those who are also in the room. This ultimately turns into a silent competition within the team. It may never be openly encouraged by the leadership, but it definitely can be an element of the culture everyone is aware of. It's not wrong to keep an eye on the dashboard and know the numbers, this can be very helpful in running a church and lead to healthy growth. It only becomes a problem when we use the numbers as our guiding tool for success. The problem is that when we operate this way our emotions will rise and fall on the numbers each week, and ministry becomes a rollercoaster ride of unhealthy emotions.

Ambition is a good thing, but when it's out of control, well, that's a whole different story. I have personally witnessed ambition trample on people to gain the next rung on the ladder. It became very real to me when I was the one getting trampled on. It's a horrible feeling knowing someone is only relating to you because they see you as a stepping stone to get something they want. But the reality is, when this is the culture we are exposed to and have been raised as leaders in, it becomes who we are. We learn to survive, and self-preservation becomes the goal. We learn quickly to elevate ourselves every chance we have because this is how we find recognition.

The reality is, God never instructed us to build churches this way. The Bible is very clear that our role is not to make the church grow. We are to plant the seed and water it, and it is God who makes it grow.

1 Corinthians 3:6 (NIV)
6. I plant the seed, Apollos watered it, but God has been making it grow.

Why is it so many of us are striving to do the growing of the church?! One of the best statements I have heard with regard to church growth which was said by John Finkelde, from *Grow a Healthy Church*, which is, 'Healthy things grow.' If we have any responsibility, it is to ensure that what we are doing is building health into the church, helping people discover how to have a holistic approach to life and ministry. If we nurture the seed and tend to the seed, making sure it has everything it needs to get established, then God will do what only He can do, which is grow His church. When I started in my new role with C3 New Hope, pastor Andrew Gray opened my eyes in this area by saying, 'We have never been told by God to preside over the growth of the church.' This means we can relax in our ambition. We don't need to work harder. It's not about doing more but rather about working smarter, and doing the right things well, which we will talk about later in this book.

CHAPTER FOUR

Being Authentically me

I AM WHO I AM

Walking this 'Better Way Journey' has empowered me to discover who I am. I've lived a great portion of my life confused about my identity and unfortunately because of this I expended a lot of energy trying to be someone who wasn't the real me. Discovering who I am, and my purpose has been a confronting process that has led me to rethink the opinion I have of myself.

There still is a lot about who I am which needs to change and that's ok. Life is not a sprint but rather a marathon. What matters most is the willingness to do whatever it takes to pursue the change and growth required to be all that God calls me to be. It didn't take long before I realised I'm not perfect. Learning to accept this fact and face the reality that I am the biggest problem in my life has been bitter sweet, but it has set me up to becoming a better person.

It has taken me many years and a lot of hard truths recognising the person I was, but I now find it exciting to peel back another layer and discover something new about the person God wants me to be. It definitely makes life interesting. The beautiful thing is I am now not trying to fabricate anything, I am simply discovering the real me. Ultimately this is the person who God is most interested in.

> *1 Corinthians 15:10 (The Passion Translation)*
> *10 But God's amazing grace has made me who I am! And his grace to me was not fruitless. In fact, I worked harder than all the rest, yet not in my own strength but God's, for his empowering grace is poured out upon me.*

What a profound revelation it is to grasp the work God has accomplished in each of us and then be content in who we are. There is rest for our soul when we are able to truly speak with honesty, "I am who I am because of the grace of God". The Apostle Paul's words have become a great comfort to me as I've progressed on this journey of discovering the new me, the real me. It's freeing to become settled in the fact I am me and I don't have to be anyone else, I have been created by God and He wants me to be the person I am.

BEING AUTHENTICALLY ME

"Who am I?" And, "What am I here for?" These have been two questions which have lived deep within me for many years. I have always struggled to understand my purpose, especially in the dark years of my life when everything seemed to be so pointless. It wasn't until I became a Christian that I started to realise there is a bigger picture for my life. I couldn't see exactly what it was, but I just knew on the inside there was more to life than I was currently experiencing.

Discovering who we are is linked to understanding our purpose. It's impossible to separate our identity and the reason we were created, because we need both revelations to live a fulfilling life.

Everybody has been created by God and has been given a unique purpose in this life. The problem is a lot of us don't realise it takes a willingness and desire in us to search out the answers to these questions.

So what's it mean to be 'authentically me?' To be authentic is to be real about who we are, no faking or facades. It's the removal of all masks and an acceptance of the person who is revealed behind the masks.

For many years I covered myself with all sorts of masks and facades. I didn't want people to see the mess in my life. Internally I was so confused about my identity. I lived with the feeling of being a fraud, covering who I really was, so that nobody would see what was going on internally. I thought I was an expert at covering up my insecurities.

I foolishly believed the lies the devil had been telling me since I was a young boy, such as, "I'm a nobody", "I would never amount to anything and would live a meaningless life with no real joy". These lies became my identity and believing them robbed me of knowing who God says I was. The lies had shaped my life for so long that my self-talk reinforced the deception.

So, if you are struggling with knowing who you are in Christ then you need to authentick you are you and that's ok! I'm not referring to the things in our lives which are unhealthy, there are always going to be behaviours in our lives we should not accept and are not truly who we are. What I'm talking about is what lies beneath all the struggles. The real you lives under the chaos and turmoil of your life and this is the person God wants to surface and get you heading on the better way journey.

God wants to set us free to delight in who he has created us to be. In the midst of the chaos of life, God calls us to live our life from the foundation of being loved and sought after. Yes, everybody is on a journey of growth. We all have behaviours that don't please and honour God, but working from a position of self-acceptance frees us to mature and grow in all areas of our lives.

IDENTITY DILEMMA

In order to understand the bigger picture of our lives, the first piece of the puzzle is discovering our identity. Identity and purpose are linked, and once we have a grasp on our identity we will almost instantly start to understand our purpose.

Discovering my identity has been a process of aligning who I am with who God says I am. The Bible is full of scriptures which describe who we have been created to be. This alignment can sometimes feel like a tug of war as we grapple with letting go of the parts of ourselves which are in conflict with who God says we are in His Word. The Bible is overflowing with descriptions of God's true intent for who we are called to be. We cannot understand our identity until we understand who God says we are. And we read about this in the Bible.

We can't figure out who we are by looking at what we do or want to do. Our identity lives at a deeper level than our title, or position, or even the calling God has placed on our lives. As you walk the 'Better Way' though, you'll discover how your title, position and the calling God has placed on our lives are intertwined.

We discover our identity not by what we know, but rather by Who we know. Who we are is found in a relationship with our Father in heaven. This is how Jesus discovered who He truly was, and this is how we will as well.

The most profound revelation I have had in regard to my identity has come from Jesus' baptism experience. This verse became the key which unlocked the door to my identity dilemma.

Matthew 3:17(NIV)
17 And a voice from heaven said, "This is my Son, whom I love; with Him I am well pleased."

This one verse has literally transformed my entire life. Since discovering I am a son of God, and that God is my Father, I have been able to break free from so much confusion. I have lost count of the amount of times I have reflected upon the truth of this one verse. I am thankful God has revealed to me my sonship, because I can now honestly say I am content in who I am. I have found great strength in understanding my true identity.

The devil cannot shake me anymore. His lies can't override the truth any longer. The authority I have discovered as a child of God has been extraordinary, not just for my life but for those God has placed under my care.

Discovering our true identity has a profound impact on our life, which is so much greater than we could ever imagine or even conceive.

If you are struggling to figure out who you are, then maybe come at it from another angle and ask yourself who you are not. This will bring fresh perspective to lead you to the answer you are seeking.

PURSUING OUR CALLING

It wasn't until I started to get a handle on my identity that I started to get a feeling for what God was calling me to. I remember that very early on in my relationship with Jesus there came a moment when I felt God speak to me so clearly about my future. I had been a Christian for about six weeks and was attending church weekly. One Sunday night in worship I felt God impress on my heart the word 'Pastor.' At the time my only understanding for this word was the pasta you find in an Italian dish. It was foreign to me. Yet it kept repeating in my mind for the whole service. After the service was finished I remember going up to my Pastor and I shared with him what I thought I heard while worshipping. As soon as I finished talking, the first thing he said to me was, "I can see Pastoring in your future; have you ever considered going to Bible college?" And this became the beginning of the journey I find myself on to this day. Eighteen years of pursuing the adventure of that one word God spoke to me: Pastor. It has significantly changed my life.

"Pastor" was, and still is, the calling and purpose God has for my life. It's not who I am, but it is definitely connected to my identity. This one word holds all of what God has for me to do. The word 'Pastor' means 'Shepherd'. The role of a shepherd is to tend and care for God's people. The calling to Pastor people is a noble cause. A Pastor is called first and foremost to be a lover of people, and we should never forget the privilege of being entrusted with the people God has placed in our flock.

All of our callings, whether you are called to be a Pastor or to something else in God kingdom, can look very different, but I can assure you of one thing; the motive underlying each calling is to be servants of the people God has trusted us with.

This is something God has so clearly spoken to me about over the last few years and has become such an important part of my philosophy of ministry by which I function. I take the calling God has given me very seriously and want to be able to stand before God when my time comes and be able to say I did the best I could with the people He gave me to care for.

Like everything we do and love, our experiences within our calling can have its good and bad moments. There have been plenty of times when I was ready to give being a Pastor away and would have been happy to pursue a career in the world. Let's face it, Pastoring isn't the best paying job in the world and most of us are volunteering more time than we are paid for. But that's the reality of our calling. It's not a career and we aren't climbing some corporate ladder. I do what I do because this is God's purpose for my life, and even though it has its moments, I love what I'm called to do. Currently I feel like I am smack bang in the middle of where I'm meant to be. I find fulfillment and value in being a Pastor and would not want to do anything else.

Two passages of scripture which have been my guiding light and have shaped my calling into what it is today are:

> *Romans 1:1 (NIV)*
> *1 'Paul, a servant of Christ Jesus, called to be an apostle and set apart for the gospel of God.'*

> *Jeremiah 1:5 (NIV)*
> *5 'Before I formed you in the womb I knew you, before you were born I set you apart; I appointed you as a prophet to the nations.'*

Both of these verses are very clear on what our calling is about, we are servants, we are called, and we are set apart. Each one of us can identify with these three distinctives of being called.

1. We are servants, and the foundation of our purpose is to serve people, not the other way around. It's sad to see when this is flipped the other way and people are used to serve us. From my experience this is when I have seen churches fall apart and people get hurt and burnt out.

2. We are called by God to people, not a career. It's not about performance or achievements. It's about people, and people should be cared for.

3. We are set apart. God has separated us from the world for His purpose. We are meant to live differently and stand out in society. The world needs contrast to be able to see the truth.

As you can see as we start to understand our calling and purpose then we are able to discover the ministry God has for us.

UNDERSTANDING MINISTRY

Our calling will inevitably lead us into the ministry God wants us to do. When hearing the word 'ministry' we can have various interpretations. A lot of people assume when hearing the word 'ministry' that it is for a select few in the church, and is practised by those who stand up the front and deliver the word of God. Sadly, this understanding is widely accepted, but is terribly unbiblical.

So, what is ministry? Ministry is the outworking of God's calling on your life. It's the legs of our purpose and can be found in many different expressions in life. Being behind a pulpit is just one expression of ministry and should never be seen as the only way God can use us to build His kingdom. The reality is, we all have a ministry from God. Often it is found in the now of our world, sometimes in our vocation and other times in our family and friendships. God has called all of us to be ministers in a harvest field which He has prepared for us ahead of time. All we need to do to discover our ministry is to be open and say 'yes' to God wherever we are right now, having the courage to look for the opportunities to share God's love with those who God brings our way.

The biggest question being answered for me at the moment in regard to ministry is how can I be the type of minister God wants me to be? Everyday I feel more and more convinced that God is asking me to lead with my heart first, with caring hands and humility.

Ministry has been an evolving journey for me. There has been a peeling of layers in my understanding of what it means to be in ministry. I am realising that all ministry is about people and should never become something that is about recognition or title. We can't climb the ladder of ministry because there is no ladder. There are no CEOs in heaven. All ministry comes from a calling which can only be delivered by God.

At its core, ministry carries the heart of a shepherd. A shepherd cares for the sheep and is led to do the things he does, to discharge his responsibilities, on behalf of the sheep. A shepherd knows his sheep and his sheep know his voice.

> *John 10:1-6 (NIV)*
> *1 'Very truly I tell you Pharisees, anyone who does not enter the sheep pen by the gate, but climbs in by some other way, is a thief and a robber.*

> *2 The one who enters by the gate is the shepherd of the sheep.*
> *3 The gatekeeper opens the gate for him, and the sheep listen to his voice. He calls his own sheep by name and leads them out.*
> *4 When he has brought out all his own, he goes on ahead of them, and his sheep follow him because they know his voice.*
> *5 But they will never follow a stranger; in fact, they will run away from him because they do not recognize a stranger's voice.'*
> *6 Jesus used this figure of speech, but the Pharisees did not understand what he was telling them.*

There is a relationship between the shepherd and the sheep. It is intimate by nature, built on trust. The sheep follow because they trust the shepherd's voice. This trust is built over time and involves the shepherd spending time in the field getting messy with the sheep's mess.

This is the role of the pastor. The pastor must smell like the sheep or he is not doing his job. We cannot claim to be a shepherd, yet never step into the field with the sheep. Pastoring cannot be done from afar because the foundation of pastoring is built on relationship. If there isn't any real relationship then the people will not trust the pastor and will easily move to another flock.

———

THE VALUE OF RELATIONSHIPS

I remember when I was just about to become the senior pastor of my first church. I had great ideas of what it would be like and how I was going to do things differently than my pastor did. I can still recall a conversation I had with him one day in the office as we were talking through the logistics of transitioning the church to my leadership. As we were talking I said, 'I am only going to connect with those who can help me build the church. I don't want to waste time on people who have nothing to offer me.' The words were so naive and immature, and I can't believe I'm writing them now. Thinking back I feel so stupid, what an idiot!

My pastor just looked at me and said, 'No you won't. That would be silly of you.' I wish I had listened to him. It would have saved me a lot of frustration over the years. I spent a lot of time trying to get the attention of people who were never going to be true friends and who had the same attitude as me.

Relationships are at the core of what God has for our future. The entire Bible can be summed up in this one word: 'relationship'. The person we are becoming is linked to the people we are connected with. Whole futures are made or broken entirely on the types of relationships that are in our lives. I've personally seen people with the greatest potential lose everything because they connected with the wrong person who led them away from their true purpose in Christ. Even to this day there is one person in particular who is still struggling to discover his purpose because of this problem. He has gone from one failed opportunity to another, chasing money and title, when he should have been pursuing the ministry call on his life. He missed it because of one relationship which led him off the right path, and into the wilderness.

I have always been very aware of the relationships I allow into my world and at times have had to make some hard decisions when it comes to who is allowed into my life.

Relationships can be tricky to navigate as a pastor, because it can be hard for people to see past our ministry role. People tend to have very high expectations of us when it comes to their interactions with us, and because of these expectations, it can be hard to know if the relationship is one where we are able to be ourselves. It's not that we present a false version of ourselves, but when you have been in ministry for an extended period of time, you learn that not everyone is a friend, and we are wise to not open our entire life to them.

To find a true friend in ministry is like finding gold. They are precious and should be held onto. I can count on my hand the real friendships I have, and almost all of them have been developed over years not weeks. I've had people who appeared to be a friend over the years - they said all the right words and acted the right way. But when the rubber hit the road, what I thought was a friendship turned out to be something different. We normally walk away from these experiences hurt and a little confused, wondering what went wrong. If it happens too many times we can find ourselves putting up walls for self-preservation and not allow anyone in. But this isn't how God wants us to deal with these situations, walls are normally erected because of fear or rejection and are not a healthy way to deal with hurt and pain in relationships. A better way is to instil appropriate, healthy boundaries which can help us move forward in a God-honoring way and will allow us to continue to have an open heart towards people. Often we build walls when we should be building fences. Fences allow us to maintain connection with the other side of the fence, walls are built to completely block out and discontinue connection. Fences are built to reveal the boundary lines and enable continued connection.

In ministry, having good friends is desperately important. Isolation is the quickest way to have your ministry fall apart. Being a pastor can be a lonely existence at the best of times, mainly because of the struggle to form true friendships. We can easily give up on trying and just walk through life with a void internally. But this isn't how God wants it to be. We were never meant to walk this journey alone and it is important for us to be intentional when it comes to building relationships in ministry.

———

- **Ministry relationships.**
Some people call this networking but for me networking is way too recognition-driven and revolves around getting the attention of the big names in the room. There isn't really any authentic relationship in networking because it's built on what I can get out of a connection.
But ministry relationships are different; I'm wanting a real connection. I interact with people with the motive to build a lasting friendship. These sorts of relationships can't be found in a short period of time but rather take investment and commitment. I also look for how a person interacts with the people in the church and look to see what kind of taste is left once they have left the conversation. I've always made decisions on ministry friendships based on how real the connection is. Below are some things I look for when building a relationship in ministry:
1. Is the person authentic?
2. Do we have a real, open and honest connection with each other?
3. What are their motives for connection?
4. Do they love people?

5. Are they interested in me and the people or just the pulpit?
6. Are they willing to return next year?
7. Have they left a deposit in the people they've connected with?

- **Personal relationship**

Finding fulfilling personal relationships as a pastor can be tricky. Often we find distance between ourselves and people. Sometimes this is because of past hurts or experiences which didn't work out that well and have left a bitter taste in our mouths. We can become cynical when it comes to finding friends and can even give up trying. There was a time when my wife and I felt this way and had settled for just having each other. Ministry can feel lonely sometimes because of the difficulties in building authentic relationships.

I'm so thankful that this season in our lives has come to an end. Looking back I realise now just how much of the disconnection and feeling of loneliness was actually my own fault. I had believed that pastors could never really have true friendships and should keep distance between themselves and the people. This is such a lie from the enemy, and it ripped me off from having many good friendships over the years.

I now find myself thinking very differently about relationships. They are essential in life and ministry, and if we don't prioritize them we will feel lonely and isolated. Close friends are like gold to me now. I value them and have made a commitment to keep the relationships alive. There is a tremendous amount of fulfillment that comes from having friends in our lives and we should never disregard the value of having a friend, and also being a friend to someone. Ministry without friends is torture. We need personal relationships desperately and should do all we can to invest in them.

- **Unhealthy relationships.**
  We should make a commitment to ourselves to either weed out unhealthy relationships or bring in stronger boundaries to lessen the impact they have on our lives. I've learnt a lot of lessons in this area of life and have had my fair share of difficult relationships. The older I get, the less tolerant I am when it comes to disrespectful or fake relationships. I honestly don't have the stomach to entertain someone who is narcissistic or manipulative. I am quick now to sever the relationship or restrict its influence in my life. I can't afford to allow a negative relationship to shape my thinking or behaviour. I have fought too long and hard in my life to be emotionally healthy and I am not willing to have to fight all over again.

  When it comes to unhealthy relationships it takes wisdom and experience to navigate the tricky waters. We shouldn't ever write people off before we get to know them, but at the same time if we become aware of a problem we should slow the pace of the relationship and limit our exposure until we have developed boundaries and considered if this relationship is needed in our lives.

———

An authentic, real friendship is the most amazing experience, and we should desire to have it because God never intended us to walk through this life alone. We are inherently social beings, which means life is enriched through the connection and relationships we form throughout our lives. When it comes to ministry too many good pastors end up ship-wrecked in their faith because they become isolated and lonely. This is a major cause of depression and mental health issues in the ministry, and is one I am super passionate about. There is a real need for those in ministry to have healthy friendships.

Many years ago I started to form a friendship with a local minister in my city. He was from a different denomination, but we got along really well, and we started to get to know each other over a period of a couple of months. After a few weeks went by I realised I hadn't heard from him and I tried to contact him. When I finally got through I discovered he was in a mental health hospital and his wife had left him because of something he had done.

When I visited him at the hospital he told me the truth about his situation. He had started drinking a lot due to the problems he was facing. Because of this downward spiral in his emotional health and the isolation he had allowed into his life he made a very unwise decision to cheat on his wife with a prostitute which caused him to lose everything.

I was totally shocked, but also felt extremely sorry for him. If only he'd had a close friend to share his struggle with, someone who could have helped him navigate his fractured thinking and find support. If only he had a real friend. Sadly, I wasn't that person due to the short time we had known each other. Ultimately he disconnected from me and stopped answering my calls, but for me it was a wake-up call to get serious about developing relationships which would be real and lasting. This is my challenge to you: get serious about building friendships, don't allow yourself to be isolated and make a commitment to never walk alone.

CHAPTER FIVE

New beginnings

EMBRACING NEW EXPERIENCES

As long as I can remember I've always been reluctant to try new things. I don't really have an adventurous bone in my body and would much prefer to watch others experience new things. I think this is why God gave me my wife. When I met Emma she loved trying new things. She had travelled overseas multiple times and had all sorts of adventures along the way. So, as we got together and started dating, I was destined at some point to be put in a position to try something new. The first time I can remember was when we were in Canada and visited Lake Louise. It was an amazing place and the scenery totally took my breath away. Every direction I looked had snow-capped mountains, beautiful lakes and buildings. When we arrived at Lake Louise, we headed directly towards the lake to see what it looked like. As we approached, Emma noticed people were walking on the ice, and instantly she wanted to do the same as everyone else. Well this was the last thing I wanted to do, and I tried everything I could think of to get out of it - to no avail. So, realising I would have to do this, I started to follow Emma and headed towards the edge of the lake. As we got closer, I looked to my right and noticed an area of the ice which had been closed as the ice was starting to melt. This just confirmed to me I was going to die from this experience. But because we were only dating at the time I didn't want Emma to think me a coward, so I pushed on.

As I took my first step on the ice I was quietly relieved the ice remained intact under my feet, and as I looked up, I could see where the other people had been walking. I encouraged myself that if I stuck to the tried and tested path on the ice then I may just get out of this with my life.

Everything was going really well, and I gained confidence the further we went. Before I knew it, we had ventured a third of the way out on the lake. It was at this point Emma turned to me and said the words every God-fearing scaredy-cat doesn't want to hear. She said, 'Lets walk out over there where nobody else has walked.' Well, internally I was completely paralysed. 'Did she just say what I think she said? Surely she can't be serious? That ice has not been tried and tested!' But once again, before I could say a word, she had already taken the first step into the unknown and was calling me to follow her. As I looked in her direction, I was having visions of me falling through the ice. I could see myself looking up from under the ice trying to scratch my way through to the air above. I was convinced this would be the end and I'd better make preparations with the Lord to move into heaven. My wife, being who she is, has always had a way of helping me try new things. She just kept encouraging me to take a step towards her, and that's exactly what I did. I felt a real sense of accomplishment that day, and walked away with a memory of experiencing something I never thought I would do in a million years.

Developing a sense of adventure and embracing new experiences makes life fun, and believe it or not, God is into fun. And if we just give it a try, we will be, too.

A few months ago, in a mentor meeting with my pastor, Andrew started talking to me about being willing to try new things. He had noticed there was a reluctance in me to try anything new, and he felt it was hindering me enjoying life. This was a challenge for me, and to be honest it still is. Adventure doesn't come naturally to me. It's something I have to push myself into. But when I am adventurous I am always surprised at the satisfaction and feeling of accomplishment I experience. I am thankful for the people in my life who love me enough to challenge me to step out of a mundane existence and step into new experiences.

DOING MORE OF WHAT YOU LOVE

It has been the journey of doing new things which has helped me discover what I love to do. Doing what we love replenishes our soul and helps us live a fulfilling life. I believe with all my heart we should all be committed to doing more of the things we love doing. I lived for years with an empty soul. I was totally taxed in my emotions and didn't even realise it. It should have been obvious to me given the extent of the depression I was experiencing, but I had stopped doing things I loved when I was a teenager and replaced them with all matter of unhealthy crutches.

One trap we can fall into is feeling that in life we are bombarded with the things we have to do. The list is long and time consuming. These 'have to's' can overrun us and make us so busy we neglect the things which make us feel happy and fulfilled. We go from day to day, week to week, and year to year with an empty soul hating what we have to do. This is no way to live, and we were never meant to live this way.

The other trap we can fall into is over spiritualizing things in our lives. We filter everything through our 'godly goggles' and categorize everything as either godly or ungodly. Many activities in and of themselves are God-neutral. God is interested in our heart in the midst of the activities we do. God is ok with us enjoying life, He is not worried about us having down time or recreational experiences which bring us joy. If we feel God is a harsh taskmaster we may believe it is wrong to enjoy certain activities.

Psalm 37:4
Take delight in the Lord, and he will give you the desires of your heart.

God is into giving us the desires of our heart so long as they align with His will and are good for us. Our lives don't have to be all about church and ministry. Actually, if this is how we think then we are setting ourselves up for a fall.

Every one of us needs time out to replenish and recharge, we need hobbies and activities that bring fun in our lives, just for the sake of having fun. I had to rediscover the things I love to do and along the way I have discovered a few more. It's funny because even writing this book is something I have discovered I really enjoy.

So, the question remains, 'What are the things you love to do? And, 'What do you need to do so you are able to do them more often?'

DISCOVERING A HEALTHY APPROACH

As with everything in life, too much of something is seldom a good thing. Pursuing a healthy approach to life is far better. Often, we are told we need to be able to live a balanced life, that everything should have checks and balances, but the more I think about this approach I realise that balance is one of those unachievable goals. We may be able to claim some form of balance when we are young and have next to no responsibilities, but as we get older and start spinning more plates you soon realise life can't be balanced, there will always be something which tips us over the edge, and we will always feel like we are letting someone or something down. I believe a better way is to discover a healthy approach to life. It's not about equal time for all, but rather quality time at the right times for all.

When we look at life through the lens of health, we are far more likely to find a sustainable groove in life. If we are consumed with pursuing balance in our life then everyone will get a piece of us, but nobody will get the best of us. We will feel like we are unable to be effective, and frustration will set in as we are pulled from pillar to post. This is the quickest way to burning out and is completely unwise.

Every situation we face in life has a healthy and an unhealthy way to deal with it and we need to choose our approach. If we are quick to confront an issue and barge in to resolve it, we will often, either by choice or by ignorance, approach it in an unhealthy way and end up saying and doing things we may regret. To face a problem in a healthy way requires us to slow down, take time to consider the problem and strategically decide on the right way to handle it, rather than barging in. This is called wisdom and is essential if we want to maintain a healthy balance.

Here are some simple questions to ask ourselves when we need to decide how to proceed which will help us choose the pathway of a healthy approach.

> What is God saying to me about the situation?
> Am I being rational in my thinking about the situation or am I over thinking?
> What are my options?
> Am I the problem?
> Do I need to talk to someone about it?
> What outcome am I believing to see?

As we slow the pace of our decision making processes, we are able to evaluate all the different angles and make an informed, well thought through decision which has considered God's perspective.

We will not always get it right, that's just being a human. But if we are willing to pursue health and be considerate of others then we will have the right motive behind our approach.

REBUILDING DEVOTION

Devotion is defined as a great love, affection and admiration for someone or thing. I love this definition. It really helps us to understand what a true devotional life is meant to be. When I went through depression, I completely lost my devotional life as I knew it. There were times when I couldn't pray and also times when I wouldn't pray. Praying and reading the Word had felt such a lifeless thing for me to do. It was almost impossible for me to focus and hold my attention on the scriptures, and when I did speak with God, I would fixate so much on deliverance and binding devils that I never stopped to actually listen to what God had to say.

Prayer had always been something I struggled with. I always felt my prayer times were disconnected and lifeless. It was rare for me to feel God's presence or hear His voice. I would often just sit there and feel like God was so distant. These experiences were a result of being a fatherless child. Having a dad who has been distant and disconnected from me for most of my life has made it difficult to understand how to relate to God as my Father.

I've had to learn what it means to interact with God as my Father, and connecting with God with the understanding that He is not like my earthly father has been a real breakthrough.

I can't give you a formula or a process for prayer and devotion. I don't have any secret revelation on how to pray or read the Word. All I can share is how God has revealed to me His Father's heart, and how embracing God as my Father has transformed my relationship with Him. I don't believe God is looking for the perfect prayer. He isn't interested in religious jargon. What he is looking for is a son or daughter who is longing to connect with Him. The key to devotion is in our approach. Approach God as your father and it will make all the difference.

*   **Discovering the Father's love.**

> *Matthew 3:17(NIV)*
> *And a voice from heaven said, "This is my Son, whom I love; with Him I am well pleased."*

I love these words God declares over Jesus, What a moment! You can imagine that Jesus hearing his Father's words would have transformed him and reassured him of his identity and purpose. Just imagine what it would have felt like to hear your father inform everyone in the crowd that He loves you and is pleased with you, before you ever achieved anything of significance. Jesus hadn't healed anyone; he hadn't preached or performed a single miracle.

It is so clear from this verse that God is not focused on performance. His love for us is not based on our ability to appease Him or accomplish anything great. We can draw great confidence from His words, that when He said, 'He loves us,' it is coming from a Father's heart. And with a Father's heart comes acceptance. Think of it from this angle. Before we ever acknowledged God or had even heard of Him, He loved us! His love for us isn't even determined by salvation! Wow! Mind blowing! God's love knows no boundaries or barriers, and He does not discriminate. You are loved, and that is the end of the story.

This verse has had a profound impact on me and has completely transformed my devotional life. Understanding this verse feels like I have discovered so much more about God. I feel like I can have a fresh beginning in my relationship with Him. It's amazing how just one scripture can have so much impact in our lives and can literally shift a lifetime of misunderstandings of who and what a Father is like.

I remember the first time I felt this scripture speak to me. I was reading through the chapter and when I got to this verse I felt it leap off the page at me. It was all I could think about. I couldn't go any further, and even today, I'm still totally mesmerised with this passage. I have always had a longing in my heart to be a son. I had a great void inside because of growing up without a father, but when I read this verse, I felt the void start to fill and a sense of the Father's love came over me. I just knew I had been made aware of God as my heavenly Father - I had encountered the Father's love!

I would read His words over and over again. I would think about them and find myself lost in what it felt like to hear them spoken over my life. I started reading the scripture and placing myself in it. I would declare it over my life, "I am my Father's son, He loves me; and He is pleased with me". The more I did this the more I felt the void on the inside fill with His love and acceptance. It is a marvellous feeling to feel the brokenness start to mend and the pain ease. I am so thankful to God for revealing Himself in this way. I am a different person today because of Him.

When we can see God as our Father then it's not hard to draw a line between what God declared over Jesus and how the father treated the lost son on his return home in the story of the prodigal son. It's such a vivid illustration of what the father's love looks like and how he feels about us, let's read through the passage and see with our own eyes just how loving our Father is.

Luke 15:11-24(NIV)
The Parable of the Lost Son
11 Jesus continued: "There was a man who had two sons.
12 The younger one said to his father, 'Father, give me my share of the estate.' So he divided his property between them.
13 "Not long after that, the younger son got together all he had, set off for a distant country and there squandered his wealth in wild living.
14 After he had spent everything, there was a severe famine in that whole country, and he began to be in need.
15 So he went and hired himself out to a citizen of that country, who sent him to his fields to feed pigs.

16 He longed to fill his stomach with the pods that the pigs were eating, but no one gave him anything.
17 "When he came to his senses, he said, 'How many of my father's hired servants have food to spare, and here I am starving to death!
18 I will set out and go back to my father and say to him: Father, I have sinned against heaven and against you.
19 I am no longer worthy to be called your son; make me like one of your hired servants.'
20 So he got up and went to his father.
"But while he was still a long way off, his father saw him and was filled with compassion for him; he ran to his son, threw his arms around him and kissed him.
21 "The son said to him, 'Father, I have sinned against heaven and against you. I am no longer worthy to be called your son.'
22 "But the father said to his servants, 'Quick! Bring the best robe and put it on him. Put a ring on his finger and sandals on his feet.
23 Bring the fattened calf and kill it. Let's have a feast and celebrate.
24 For this son of mine was dead and is alive again; he was lost and is found.' So they began to celebrate.

This passage is rich with descriptions of who the father is, and how he interacts with his son. It's such a profound revelation and one we all need to embrace. Understanding the Father helps us know how to be a son and gives us confidence in our relationship with Him. Below are some of my reflections on the Father and what I have experienced with him.

———

*   **Our father will wait for us to come to him.**

Luke 15:20(NIV)
20 So he got up and went to his father.
"But while he was still a long way off, his father saw
him and was filled with compassion for him; he ran
to his son, threw his arms around him and kissed
him.

The one thing I have come to realise about God is thatHe is very patient with us. He is in no hurry when it comes to us spending time with Him, and will wait as long as it takes for us to come to Him. God is looking out for us all the time, His heart longs for us and he has all the time in the world to spend time with us.

*   **Our father will never turn his back on us.**

Luke 15:20(NIV)
20 So he got up and went to his father.
"But while he was still a long way off, his father saw
him and was filled with compassion for him; he ran
to his son, threw his arms around him and kissed
him.

I love this thought about God; He is always faced towards us. Our Father is always looking out for us and is facing in our direction. I can just imagine the father in this story standing outside everyday looking in his son's direction, waiting for the slightest indication of the son's return. The father always believed, and held onto the hope, that his son would one day come home, and he wanted to be the first to welcome him back and reinstate him into the family.

God will never forsake us, because He forsook Jesus. God turned His back on Jesus when he was on the cross, so that He would never have to turn His back on us. This means we will never be turned away or forgotten by God. God is waiting every day for us to turn to Him and head in His direction.

*   **Our Father embraces us in our mess.**

> *Luke 15:20(NIV)*
> *20 So he got up and went to his father.*
> *"But while he was still a long way off, his father saw*
> *him and was filled with compassion for him; he ran*
> *to his son, threw his arms around him and kissed*
> *him.*

The Father is not afraid of mess. The son wasn't in a good way when he returned home. He had ended up feeding pigs in a pig pen, he smelt like pigs and looked like the pen, covered in mud and slop. This was the reality of the son's appearance when the father saw him at a distance, yet this didn't deter him from running and embracing his son.

Understanding the culture of the time here is important because it paints a clear picture of just how much the father was willing to do for his lost son. There are two cultural norms the father ignores. Firstly, pigs were deemed unholy and were prohibited by Jewish law, which means the son was judged as unclean by law and would have been expected to be cleansed before re-entering the community. This doesn't stop the father though, he loved his son so much that he was willing to overlook this cultural rule and embraced his son anyway. Secondly, it was considered undignified for a father to run to a son in their culture. The fact that the father was willing to be seen as undignified before his peers, and embrace his unclean son, is a beautiful picture of just how much God loves us and the price He was willing to pay to accept us as His sons and daughters.

Often, we think that what we have done can make God not want to touch us, that we are untouchable in God's eyes. But this is a lie. All of us at some point lived in our own mess, and we live with the smell of what we have done until we come to God and sort it with Him. Yet this never determines God's willingness to love us and embrace us. The truth is, without God embracing us in our mess we can never become clean. His embrace is the first step of our restoration.

*	**Our father hears our confession but focuses on resto ration.**

> *Luke 15:21-22(NIV)*
> *21 "The son said to him, 'Father, I have sinned against heaven and against you. I am no longer worthy to be called your son.'*
> *22 "But the father said to his servants, 'Quick! Bring the best robe and put it on him. Put a ring on his finger and sandals on his feet.*

Confessing our sins and mistakes is more to do with us rather than God. When we sin, we are the one who causes separation in our relationship with our Father. Sin doesn't cause God to pull away from us but rather us to pull away from Him. When we come to God and confess our sin and repent, God instantly extends forgiveness and moves on. His focus is always on our restoration and, just like the father in the passage of scripture, God is keen to reinstate us to our rightful place in the family.

Never think you have sinned so badly that God will not accept you back. God is more interested in his relationship with you than anything else.

*   **Our father loves us as his son.**

Luke 15:24(NIV)
24 For this son of mine was dead and is alive again;
he was lost and is found.' So they began to celebrate.

I love that in all that has happened in the son's life the father never once disowns or disengages from his son, even though the son disowns him. This is how the Father interacts with us. We are his children and he will never disown us. God is infatuated with us and is proud to call us His children. This is the heart of a true father; the son was willing to settle for the position of a servant but the father was unwilling to have the son in any role other than what he was born into - a son. And the same goes for us. We are his children and that is final.

———

Now I understand just how entwined God has been in my life, and how active He was through the depression and my recovery. Even in my darkest moments when I felt so alone and lost, my Father was right there beside me. He knew my pain and could empathise with what I was going through. I have a Father who was familiar with brokenness.

So, what does my devotional life look like today? Well I wouldn't say it is anything spectacular. I may never be talked about in history books as the great prayer warrior of our time. I am well aware there are people who are way more committed and gifted in prayer and devotion than I am, but I'm ok with that. I am not intimidated or concerned with someone else's sacrifice or desire for God. I am comfortable in my own skin and settled with how I spend time with my Father. It's not a competition. I don't always have the right words, or know how to pray when I sit in my quiet time with God, but that's ok, because I know my Father delights in every minute I spend in his company. He is pleased with me before I say a word, and He is pleased with me even if I don't say anything at all. God doesn't get angry if I miss a time of prayer, and He doesn't reject me because I have allowed busyness to distract me. He just waits with a longing heart until I come to Him, and when I do, He celebrates our communion.

I feel like I have discovered a sweet spot in my devotional life, a place of contentment and rest with God. A place where I can just be me, His son, and know that God is ok with who I am. From this position he can start to mould my life the way a Father moulds a son. So, my devotional life is developing and I am growing in my desire to spend more time with God. I don't always get it right, but I'm heading in the right direction, and that's ok.

CHAPTER SIX

The Comeback

THE COMEBACK

Coming back into a broader ministry environment has been difficult for me. I find myself with little to no patience for the fluff some people go on with when it comes to ministry and church growth. The jostling for recognition and approval has become so visible to me and I have often avoided certain settings because of it. Sometimes I think I should force myself to adjust to the environment, but this would just be undoing everything God has done in me over the last few years. God hasn't brought me this far so I can just fall back into old patterns of behaviour. I know that what God has done in me is for a greater purpose which I am yet to discover. And what I have experienced and walked through with God will be a great help for others who, like me, are hungry for change and a better way.

I love the idea of a comeback. It's a theme we see often in movies. The guy who was successful and on top of the world is defeated and hits rock bottom, only to find he is given another chance to come back, but this time with greater wisdom and determination. God is the God of the comeback. I tell my church all the time that God is not the God of a second chance but rather the God of another chance. He is into the comeback and is our greatest encouragement inspiring us to get up and give it another shot.

It can be hard to find the faith to get up and go again, to move beyond the past and be willing to let go of the hurt and pain. But we have to decide what's more important to us, holding onto something which will anchor us in the past, or grabbing hold of what lies in the future? The reality is we can't have both. Having our anchor down and our sail up will only cause tension which will rip us apart.

Just like in the movies, the key to a great come back is discovering a new purpose - finding a reason to fight which is greater than the original purpose. When we are able to identify our reason to fight then we are able to get up again and have our comeback. This time though, things will be different, because we have a different motivation. When I was coming back from depression my reason to fight was my children, they were my motivation. Now that I am coming back into the ministry arena my reasons to fight are for those who are suffering in silence and can't see a better way forward. I want to take God's redemption story of overcoming weakness in my life and give it to those who are drowning in despair. My ultimate goal is to see others succeed where they have failed in the past, to see them winning in life again.

RENEWED PURPOSE

I have a renewed purpose in God. My desire is to see change happen in the church and for a new breed of pastor to rise up who will restore the 'balance of the force' to the ministry. For too long the focus on 'leadership at all costs' has left a trail of broken and worn out people. Good people have been left behind because the pace has been set at unsustainable levels, and the shepherd has been overlooked for the 'superstar' who can tick all the boxes of performance. Church has become about pursuing the vision at all costs. This has led to a culture of performance, and an unhealthy desire to use people as a commodity to make the vision happen. Surely this is not what Jesus meant when He said, 'He would build the church.' Is it possible we have wandered from the path which was laid out for us?

We need a better way, a way in which people are not a commodity to be used for the vision but rather people are the vision. I am praying for the day the Shepherd leader stands up again and embraces the call of God to care for His people. I often wonder what God would say to some of us who have been so focused on performance and producing results that we have lost sight of what God really is concerned about, the very reason why He sent His son to die for us in the first place.

I felt led to write this book to challenge those who read it to reflect and consider their approach in ministry and to ask themselves the question, 'Is there a better way?' - a way in which there is a healthy approach which produces good fruit.

Identifying the new purpose is vital for our comeback. It is the rudder that directs our course and helps us stay on our true north. We should know our purpose so well that we are able to sum it up in one word. For me the one word is 'legacy'. I want to leave a legacy of a transformed life. I will talk about this at the end of this chapter in more detail.

So, the question remains. What is your renewed purpose? Are you able to define it in one word? It is so important to take the time to clarify this. It will become your driving motivator for the way ahead and will be very different from any path you have walked before. Take some time to seriously consider and ponder the question, it will be well worth the time and effort.

NEW AGENDA

I have a very simple agenda these days. I have learnt the hard way that there are things which only God can do, and they are not for me to interfere with. For instance, only God can grow His church! It is not my role to grow the church. My job is to plant and water the seed, but it is God's job to bring the increase.

> *1 Corinthians 3:6*
> *'I planted the seed, Apollos watered it, but God has been making it grow.'*

Once I understood this principle I started to relax and do things differently. My agenda is to love God's people and pastor them well. I no longer apply pressure to peoples' worlds so we can achieve the next big goal. I've learnt to work with where people are at in their availability and commitment. This can be difficult at times, but I'm ok with living with a little frustration every now and then. I often remind myself that I'm here to serve people, not the other way around.

I now consider myself to be a shepherd-leader and have settled into the zone of caring for the flock God has given me, and to lead them with integrity of heart. I'm willing to lead a little slower and be patient. I don't want to get to the end and realise I have left people behind who should be with me because I was unwilling to wait for them. If this means the church won't be the largest in town, then that's ok. I suspect time will prove me right in what I'm feeling from God, and this approach will not affect the growth of the church but rather strengthen it.

There are no hidden agendas in my life anymore. I am not trying to impress anyone or out-do another pastor. I refuse to play the comparison game and there is nothing in me anymore that wants to wear a facade. My church is what it is, and I am who I am, unapologetically. Do I want the church to grow? Yes! Do I want to see people get saved? Yes! I want to see all the same things every pastor wants to see, but I will not allow these things to be my driving motivator for what God wants me to do. My motivation is simply to love God, love the people, and love what I do. That's it! Anything else is outside my jurisdiction.

Life becomes simple when you realise God is not expecting us to be something we are not. When our agenda aligns with God's, there is a simplicity in everything we do.

LIVING INSIDE OUT

When we know what we value most, it creates a renewed internal culture, which impacts our behaviours. Values will always determine the culture that is established internally and externally. What we value will direct our decisions, and how we implement those decisions. Our actions are an outworking of the value system which is embedded in us. Some of what we do has been passed down from our families, and other behaviours are imparted through the influence of the social environments we travel in such as church, school, university, other religious organisations, peer groups, and the list goes on. All of these areas can influence our internal culture. Often we don't even realise how deeply ingrained these values are in us until they are challenged, which is exactly what happens when we become a Christian.

When we say 'Yes' to Jesus, we are saying 'Yes' to the Kingdom of God. Through this decision we accepted the culture of heaven and made a commitment to live our lives the way God intended for us to live. To do this we need to allow God to rewire our internal life and sift out the things which do not align with His Kingdom culture. This can be a challenging process and experience which can cause a complete upheaval in our identity and purpose in life.

For me this process drilled deep down into the core of who I was. God challenged my perceptions about myself, and I had to discover who I really was in Him. Once He shifted my identity He then focused on the motives of my heart and the way I interacted with people. By the time He had finished with me I felt like a completely different person, and I am better for all He has done.

I now live with a transformed internal culture. My motives now come from a much deeper understanding of who God is and who I am. The way I minister to people and lead them comes from a more real, authentic place in my spirit and soul. Almost all the confusion I once carried has been resolved, and I am confident in what God has asked me to do and how He wants me to do it. It feels like I'm in my sweet spot for the first time in my life and I love it.

It's amazing how fulfilling life can be when there is no longer an internal battle raging, when you are able to stand before God and man confidently and comfortably in who you are, knowing you are not perfect, yet you are fully accepted by your Father in heaven. This is the internal culture I am talking about. It directs our lives and moulds our futures.

Experiencing this shift internally doesn't just happen. We have to be willing to engage with the process of allowing God to tinker with our insides and rearrange things as He wants to. This can be uncomfortable at times as we become aware of our weaknesses and failings. But if we are willing to engage with God and walk the journey, we will come out the other side far more prepared and equipped for what God is going to do in and through us.

LEAVING A LEGACY

One of the biggest changes I recognise in me is thinking in the present, while also holding the end-picture in mind. I feel like my focus has shifted and the future is not solely about me anymore. There is a much more important mission at hand than my own success and it is a burden that is growing in my heart. I have a responsibility to leave a legacy on this earth and an inheritance for my children.

> *Proverbs 13:22 (NIV)*
> *A good person leaves an inheritance for their children's children. But a sinner's wealth is stored up for the righteous.*

I have a driving desire to leave a legacy in people's lives. I never thought I would experience this desire so early in my life. I've always believed I would be concerned more about leaving a legacy when I am in my 70's, yet here I am in my 40's feeling a strong burden to impart and father those God brings my way. I want to have a lasting impact on those around me, especially those who are struggling like I have in ministry. I believe God has allowed me to travel through all that has taken place in my life for such a time as this.

A legacy is a gift we give to the next generation. A legacy is significant because those who give it have paid a hefty price to attain it, and so it holds great value. The greatest legacy any of us can receive is what God has made available to us through His son - salvation. Salvation came at a great cost to God. The sacrifice of His son Jesus was the highest price tag which has ever existed, and one God was willing to pay for you and me.

> **John 3:16 for God so loved the world that He gave his one and only son so whoever will believe in Him will not perish but have eternal life.**

Think about this for a minute. God found us worthy of investment. His love for us was so great he was willing and prepared to pay whatever the cost to give us a legacy. If God was willing to pay such a price for me and give me salvation, then how can I not in a similar way sacrificially invest in those God has entrusted me with? It would be a tremendous loss to get to the end of my life and realise I had wasted every opportunity to be generous with my legacy. I feel more now than ever the responsibility God has given me to pass on every lesson I have learnt from every battle I have fought. Otherwise all of it was for nothing and I have endured suffering with no lasting result.

We need to take the time to ask ourselves what kind of legacy we want to leave. Without a clear picture of what it looks like we will struggle to be able to be intentional in imparting it.

––––––

Three areas of legacy I want to be remembered for:

*   **Family**

Other than God, my family is the most important part of my life. My kids are valuable to me and there isn't anything I wouldn't do for them. They are my greatest legacy and I am very aware of the responsibility I have before God to raise them in the ways of the Lord, and also to impart wisdom for life to them. I want to leave them a legacy of how to live life well. I also want them to be able to look back and see they were loved by their earthly father. So, this gives me a clear mandate to make sure I prepare them to live their best life.

I've seen it written, 'The greatest legacy a man can leave his children is to love their mother.' I love this quote because it resonates with me, especially with my boys. I want them to grow up respecting and treating women well, and I know it's on me to show them how. I also want my daughter to understand her intrinsic worth and how a man should treat her. As a father I am also responsible to be an example for her and I know all of these lessons are learnt in how I treat their mother. If they see their mother is highly valued and highly respected by me then I have won half the battle and have given them a legacy they can continue in their lives, and their children's lives.

The most important thing I can leave my kids, though, is to show them how to love the Lord; how to live the Christian life as a true believer. It's my job to raise them in the things of the Lord and teach them how to live a devoted life. This is my highest priority for them,and if I get to the end of my life and know my kids and grandkids are living for Jesus then I feel I will have discharged my responsibility well, and my legacy would be the one I dreamt of.

*   **Ministry**

I've always had a heart to see peoples' lives transformed by God. It is one of the greatest privileges to have the opportunity to journey alongside someone as they walk the pathway of discovering who Jesus is, and experience His transformational love. It's such an honour to be used by God in this way and it is a passion of my heart to experience this more and more. When it comes to ministry I want to leave a legacy of transformed lives. I want people to be able to look back over the past and say, "Dave loved those God entrusted to him, and people are different because of the influence he had in their lives."

I would be satisfied to be remembered as a good man who lived his life serving the Lord. I don't need to have pages written about me in the history books or be remembered for any great miraculous feat. I'm not interested in fame, stature or wealth. I just want my legacy to be as simple as the ministry I believe God has given me - love God and love people. If I can achieve this in the years I have left on this earth, then I'm ok and will be a happy man ready to go home to be with Jesus.

*   **Reputation**

When I say reputation, I'm referring more to the reputation I will leave behind when I'm gone. What will I be remembered for? What do I want people to say about me? These are interesting questions to ponder.

I've sat in on, and officiated, many funerals while being a pastor. Everyone of them has been unique, ranging from experiencing deep hopelessness to leaving the funeral filled with hope. Some have been a morbid experience focused on the loss of life and the hopelessness of death, and others have been a celebration of life. Despite this, all of them have one thing in common; there is always a moment when you get a picture of who the person was and the way they lived their life. Someone will get up and give a eulogy and will talk about the memories and great things that happened in the life of the person. I believe the greatest eulogies are the ones which describe who the person was and what they lived for, where it moves past just recalling events that took place and goes a little deeper into the life they lived. I love hearing about the convictions someone lived by, their faith and the impact they had in people's lives.

Lately, funerals have started to make me think a lot about what I want my eulogy to say. What reputation will I leave behind, and will I be remembered in my family for generations to come? My hope is to leave behind a legacy for my grandchildren's children, especially with regard to their faith and their love for the Lord. I pray the impact of the decision I made 18 years ago will continue through the generations and will have a lasting impact on my family line.

Even now as I write this I am thinking about the statement on my headstone. What one statement will sum up my life and reveal my reputation to those who read it? We will all one day have our lives summed up like this and it should matter to us what our headstone will say. King David's life was summed up in the book of Acts very clearly, which reveals his reputation and legacy.

Acts 13:22 (NIV)
After removing Saul, he made David their king. God testified concerning him: 'I have found David son of Jesse, a man after my own heart; he will do whatever I want him to do.'

If David had a headstone we could read today, it would say "David was a man after God's own heart." David lived approximately 1000 years before the book of Acts was written. He experienced many failures and mistakes in his life, yet when spoken about by someone looking back on this side of his history, they sum up his reputation and legacy as a man after God's heart. Profound and thought provoking!

Let me ask you a question, 'What will people say about you a thousand years from now or even a hundred years from now?' Would you be remembered as a man who loved the Lord and lived your life for His kingdom? Would you be described as a good husband or wife? A devoted parent who was involved in and there for your children?

Let me leave you with this challenge, what would you say about yourself if you wrote your own eulogy and headstone? Take some time and consider the answer; maybe write it down on paper. How would you sum up your reputation and legacy? What one statement would you use on your headstone which would describe to people generations from now the kind of person you were?

> Here is what I would want my eulogy to say:
> 'David was a son, a husband and a father.
> He lived his life with deep conviction and love for the Lord,
> David was generous in giving the gift of healing and freedom
> Which he experienced in his own life with those who were hurting and broken.
> David loved his wife and children well with integrity and character,
> He will be remembered as a great example of an imperfect man

Who was humble in repentance and generous in grace.
His testimony is one of God's goodness and faithfulness.
He loved the Lord, his family and people deeply.
David was a man after God's own heart.'

This is what I would want my headstone to say:

He loved God and people with a heart touched by God.

CHAPTER SEVEN

Mentoring

MENTORING

So what is mentoring? Mentoring to me is the privilege of walking the journey with somebody. Having a mentor has been something I have longed for since I stepped into ministry. I've always liked the idea of having someone in my world who will not just tell me what I want to hear, but rather what I need to hear. I prayed for a long time for God to give me a mentor. I knew I needed someone, but I was never sure how to find that person and what it would be like once they were in my life.

Generally finding a mentor isn't something we just chance upon. We must be intentional when looking for the right person. Wisdom is key in this process. Remember you are going to open your life to the person so they need to be someone you can trust. Trust is given but it's also earned. You will know from the first meeting whether this relational transaction is flowing or not.

I have been blessed to have two great mentors in my life and both of them have played a significant role in helping me grow into the person I am today. Without their input and guidance I don't believe I would be as far down the pathway God has for me. Everything I am writing has come from their example and the things I have gleaned from my times with them. If there is one idea I want you to catch in all that I have said it would be this: mentors are worth their weight in gold! Do whatever it takes to find one, and open your life up to their influence. Only a fool believes they can hold it all together by themselves.

Finding a mentor and knowing what to look for can be challenging, so I thought it would be helpful to give some thoughts around the process I went through in finding my own. This is not by all means an exhaustive list, but it may help get the ball rolling and give some direction to head in so you don't have to stumble around in the dark.

WHY DO I NEED A MENTOR?

I came to the realisation I needed a mentor early on in ministry. I started to become aware of the weaknesses I had and was at a loss to know how to move forward in these areas. From then on, I was on the hunt for the right person to fill the role for me. It took me a long time to realise the person I was looking for was going to be harder to find than I believed it should be.

I was looking in the wrong places with the wrong motives. I was looking for a coach instead of a mentor and because of this I kept approaching the wrong people. Don't get me wrong, the people I was spending time with were accomplished ministers who gave me great insight into leadership and ministry. The problem was I needed something deeper than they could give me, and they couldn't give it to me because they were lacking the same thing in their life.

We need to be clear why we want a mentor in the first place. Understanding our why will lead us to the who, and this was the area I hadn't figured out. For me it all came together after my second break down. It was at this point I got a very clear understanding about what it was I wanted and who could help me get there. My prayer is for you to never have to experience the journey I went through to get the answer you need to get started.

————

So why do you need a mentor? What a great question to ask and one I'm glad we have gotten to. Below are a few reasons why we need a mentor:

- **A mentor sees the blind spots we do not see.**
  All of us have things in our lives we don't see about ourselves. They are more often than not the things that are blockages in our world. Why we don't see them sometimes can't be answered. Maybe we don't want to see it because of the pain we will experience if we actually deal with it, so out of self-preservation and protection we ignore it. Or maybe we are totally unaware of the blind spot. Either way a mentor has eyes we do not have and can see what we do not see. This can save us years of trying to figure out why we are the way we are, and it can also save us thousands of dollars in counselling dealing with mental health issues which arise from the struggle.
- **A mentor carries wisdom we do not carry.**
  The greatest mentors are those who have lived life and have succeeded, and failed, along the journey. This type of person carries an immense amount of wisdom which can be

invaluable in our own lives. Often when we are young we lack the wisdom and experience needed to make the right decisions about our future, This is where a mentor can really help empower us to move forward. They can save us a lot of hurt, pain and regret - if we are willing to listen and act upon their input.

- **A mentor has life experience we do not have.**
Believe it or not, life experience often trumps head knowledge. Most of the time theory lacks the information that only experience can give us. That's why it is so beneficial to have someone who has been there and done it, and is willing to share their life experience with us.
- **A mentor holds a key to the future of our life.**
One of the reasons we can't figure all of our life out alone is because God has given people keys to our lives that we can't get access to without coming into relationship with them. From the very beginning God has destined us to be in a relationship with other people and has locked our future up in these connections. A mentor is just one example of God using someone to further our life direction. It's really about us pursuing these relationships to discover what is hidden for our future.
- **A mentor has paid a price we are yet to pay.**
All good mentors have one thing in common - they have all paid a price to be where they are at in life. I haven't met a mentor yet that hasn't had to walk through some form of suffering and battle in their life. Their suffering and battle experiences are what qualifies them to mentor others and is where they draw from for wisdom and faith when imparting into our lives. There is a connection between the price they have paid and the impact they have: the greater the price, the deeper the impact.

———

Hopefully these reasons will help you understand why having a mentor is such an important element in our lives. If we want to live the life God has intended us to live and if we aim to find wholeness and fulfillment in life, then I know the pursuit of finding a mentor is a worthy and noble adventure, and one that is so desperately needed in this day and age.

WHERE DO I FIND A MENTOR?

Mentors are all around us, we just need to identify them. The best way to find a mentor is to reflect upon our own lives and discover the areas we want to grow in. Once we are clear about what we want then we can start looking for the person who is successful in these areas and we can ask them to invest into our lives and help us grow.

I've heard it said many times that a mentor can be someone we watch from afar, but personally I have found this to not be true. These people we are looking at may be great men and women of God, they may have significant runs on the board, and we may be able to learn a lot from them, but they are not our mentors.

Mentors are not far off in the distance of our life; they are not disconnected from us. Mentors know us and have a heart to see us grow. Mentors are willing to get involved in our mess and are not afraid to speak truth and challenge who we are and what we do.

Most of the time you will find the person you are looking for is already in your world. You may have never thought of them in this way before but if you bring your desire before God and allow Him to guide you, then you may be surprised by who He shines His light on.

So, the question isn't, 'Where can I find a mentor?' but rather, 'God, show me the person you have placed in my life to be a mentor to me.'

Prayer is something that we cannot afford to neglect in the process. Ultimately the whole venture should be immersed in prayer. Having a conversation with God and getting His direction about who we should approach to be our mentor is the most important element of making the right decision.

WHAT DOES A MENTOR LOOK LIKE?

Understanding what mentoring is meant to look like is helpful as we start the journey towards finding someone to fill this role. I have been in a lot of different environments over the years from secular business to church leadership, so I have seen the good and the bad when it comes to mentoring and coaching people for growth.

The first thing we need to understand is that there's a significant difference between mentoring and coaching. Both roles are important and necessary in our life but both have very different approaches and outcomes which we need to understand. A lot of leaders don't know how to distinguish between the two and end up spending valuable time focusing on the wrong approach and wondering why they are not seeing the results.

Let me explain the difference:

Coaching is a performance-based approach. A coach is focused on the elements of someone's life that will enhance their performance. A coach is all about working harder and striving for the result. They focus on the nitty gritty things that will draw out a little bit more performance from us to gain a better result. A great example of this would be to look at the controversies we see in professional sports. Almost weekly we are seeing young men making unwise decisions which lead them to unacceptable behaviour, both in their private and public lives. These young men and women have great talent and unbelievable potential for the future. They have been trained by the best coaches in the business, which is why they are at such elite levels in their sport. Yet, we often see the fractures in their character; something is amiss in their lives. Why do we see this so often? Is it the coach's fault? No, I don't think this is the case. A coach's role is not to guide character, but rather to guide performance. A coach is not there to deal with character flaws, and although some coaches do spend time on this area of an athlete's life, it's not their priority.

This can be the same in the church leadership arena. There are many coaches in the current church leadership environment. Everyone wants to know how to get to the next level, so we attend all sorts of conferences about how to break numerical growth barriers. There is no shortage of growth experts out there telling us we need to do this and that, and everything in between, if we want a large church. These speakers have all the right words and best strategies, and can show us all the statistics to back it up. We invite these growth experts into our churches, we have lunch with them and allow them to coach us. We believe we are being mentored but we are not. See, this person's role is to coach. When we sit with them they are showing us strategies and things we can do to increase performance because that is what they are there to do. The issue is, we put an unrealistic expectation on someone because we've misunderstood the difference between a coach and a mentor. Part of the problem is the current culture we are in regarding church leadership. Everything in the church environment is screaming leadership, growth, numbers. We become caught up hearing it from every angle which has conditioned us to think this is the way things should be, fracturing our understanding of what it means to be mentored.

On the other hand, mentoring takes a completely different approach. A mentor is invested in the private and public life of a person and is focused on developing character and integrity. When we sit with a mentor, they are not just looking at our performance and critiquing us from facts and figures, they are looking deeper and going under the surface of the facade everybody sees. The greatest mentors are readers of people. They have an ability to see the things in our lives we are unable or unwilling to see. They don't come with the latest, greatest strategies or the best programs for growth. They don't need to come with all those strategies because that is not their role. As Paul Scanlon says, 'Great mentors are fluent in human, they help us understand the language of our soul.'

So when looking for a mentor, it is vitally important we understand the difference between the two roles. This will alleviate a lot of frustration in both the mentor and mentee. We need to get clear about what outcome we are looking for and identify those people we can approach to get the ball rolling.

Things to look for in a mentor:
- Godly wisdom
- Life experience
- A love for people
- A heart for Jesus
- A transparent life
- Character and integrity
- Genuine interest in you as a person

THE POWER OF MENTORING

I have been completely amazed at the transformation I have experienced in my life since being mentored. There are things I've learnt about myself I didn't realise were in me and I have become a different person because I have allowed my mentor access to my life.

Like most things in life, you only get out of something that which you are willing to put in. The same is true when it comes to mentoring. If we are willing to jump in boots and all, then we will see great growth in our lives.

*   **Commit to being an open book**

The truth is, a mentor really doesn't have any power to change our lives, but once again that is not his role. His role is to highlight the things which are holding us back and to encourage us to do something about it. So, at the end of the day it is up to us if we are willing to change. The real power in mentoring is found in the bond between the mentor and mentee. If a relationship is strong enough then it will result in positive influence which will inspire the mentee to take action for change.

The other contributing factor we would be foolish to ignore in a mentor relationship is God. God's role in the process of change in someone's life exceeds the ability of any man to affect change, yet surprisingly God often chooses to work through people in the change process. Mentoring is at its most powerful when God is first and foremost in the discussion. When a mentor becomes a vessel for God to move through, then the mentee will experience not just the knowledge of transformation, but also the power for transformation to take place.

When we understand how God chooses to work, then we are able to see the importance a mentor has in the process of us pursuing what God has planned for our lives.

***   Never come unprepared**

Never come unprepared to a mentoring meeting or moment. If the mentor gives you some homework or encourages you to do something, then make a decision before you leave the meeting to go and do it. There is nothing more satisfying for a mentor than when we come back to our next catchup and can honestly say we have done what they have encouraged us to do and things are changing because of it.

Every time we meet with our mentor, we should have already thought through the things we feel we need direction in. This is where self-awareness comes into play, which I spoke about in a previous chapter. Don't allow it to solely be the mentor's job to address every issue in your life. Come ready to share the challenge so the mentor can focus on giving wisdom and advice which can help bring change.

Transparency is the key to being mentored. If we are unwilling to be real and open about who we are and allow our mentor to impart their wisdom and experience to us then we are wasting their time and we should end the relationship. It would be better for both parties for the mentor to move on to someone who will value and embrace their investment.

***   Always show gratitude.**

Make a commitment to always be thankful and show gratitude for the time invested and the input you receive from your mentor. Remember, they are normally busy people with multiple roles and responsibilities, and their time is valuable to them. A mentor invests and expects to see a return. Don't ever think they are under obligation to be our mentor. We must understand they choose to be in our world, which means we are the ones responsible to take on board their input and apply it to our lives. Appreciation goes a long way in saying thank you. Find out what they like and bless them with a gift, write a card to show how much you value them, or simply say thank you every time you meet. All these things will help show your gratitude and appreciation for the time and energy they give.

BECOMING A MENTOR TO OTHERS

The ultimate goal regarding mentoring is to just not be mentored yourself, but to become a mentor to others. As I get older, I see a need in peoples' lives for mentoring, and there is a growing desire in me to be a person they can turn to.

When we get to a certain age life shifts and it becomes more about the legacy we are leaving and imparting into others. I feel like I have arrived at this stage earlier than I expected. There is a growing burden in me to pursue this as I see a lost generation of leaders and pastors hungry for a better way of doing things but not finding the pathway forward in those who have gone before them.

So how do we become a mentor to others? It's not as difficult as you may think. Essentially, to be a mentor takes a willingness to make ourselves available to those around us and to be someone they can turn to for wisdom and encouragement. It's not about having all the answers. Most of the time people just need a safe sounding board to be able to process their thoughts.

So, what things can we do to become a mentor to others?
- Show interest in others.
- Be available.
- Learn to listen.
- Be willing to share your life, successes and failures.
- Allow people into your world, do life with people.
- Be a learner.
- Find a mentor for yourself.

———

Becoming a mentor is a noble cause. The world needs more people who are willing to invest in others and to be a source of encouragement for generations to come. We have a responsibility to pass on wisdom before we leave this world. It would be a great shame to have lived our whole life and to have experienced all we have walked through and to never take the time to pass on what we have learned. What an opportunity we have to build a platform for the next generation to build upon. All it takes is a willingness and desire to leave a legacy.

CHAPTER EIGHT

Where do we go from here?

WHERE DO WE GO FROM HERE?

Now that you have finished reading the book, the next logical question is, 'What now?' Well, your next step is simple. It's time to apply what you have read to your life. Every journey starts with someone taking the first step and then another, and another, until there is momentum. The first step is always the hardest, and it can take courage to motivate yourself. But know that I am your greatest fan. I'm cheering you on, and praying for you to overcome.

STEPS ON THE JOURNEY:

*   **Step one - Give yourself permission to change**

A great mentor I had many years ago said these words to me, 'Tell your head to give your heart permission to receive from God'. It has stuck with me ever since, and I often use this encouragement when I am preaching. Let me echo these words to you right now with a slight twist, 'Tell your head to give your heart permission to change!'

Often our biggest hurdle to changing is ourselves. We can get stuck in self-doubt and struggle to believe it's possible to change, but the reality is that change is a decision, and we have to choose change before we can step into it. Don't allow stinking-thinking to rob you of the life God so desperately wants you to live. Our minds are subject to our control, not the other way around. So start being the boss when it comes to the thoughts that enter your mind.

*** Step two - One step at a time**

Don't get overwhelmed by the number of things you have identified while reading this book that may need to change in your life. Whenever we read a book like this, we are inundated with a tsunami of self-awareness, and everything that is wrong becomes very visible. It's ok to switch off the alarm bell. The alarm bell is normal, especially if this is the first time you are thinking this way.

When I started down this' better way' pathway, everything was screaming at me, and all I could focus on was the mountain of impossibility before me. As I worked though with my psychologist and mentors, I started to realise the only way forward was to pick one thing and work on it. Remember every journey starts with one step and continues with one step at a time.

*** Step three - Don't do it alone.**

If I have one encouragement for you, it is to not do this journey alone. There will be a temptation to sort your life out by yourself, but let me tell you, it is not wise to open the box without the right people around you. One of the greatest lessons I have learned is that I need people in my life to help me. I didn't start this way, though, and paid the price for my foolishness. It wasn't until I opened up and sought the right support that my life started to change for the better. Opening up to people about what you are going through, finding the right mentor and professional help is all part of the process and needs to be taken seriously.

Most importantly, include God in it all. Make Him the centre of everything and allow God to lead you to the right people. Never walk alone!

***   Step four - You have what it takes.**

"You have what it takes". It's time to start believing in yourself and trusting God's word about who you are. One of the greatest quotes I have ever seen was spoken by Sir Winston Churchill, 'Never ever give up!' It was this tenacity and determination which ultimately led to the allied forces' victory and the downfall of Nazi rule throughout Europe.

We cannot afford to allow self-doubt and hopelessness to deter us from pursuing the better way God has for us. So be strong and courageous, despite the obstacles you are facing, and run your race to win. Never give up!

***   Step five - Keep fueling the fire.**

In this final step I want to give you some resources which have been instrumental in helping me keep learning and being inspired to pursue the "Better Way Life". Each resource has been a huge part of the journey and has been used by God to transform my thinking and understanding about what it really means to be human and also a Pastor.

Books:

- **The Way of the Shepherd.** *By Dr. Kevin Leman & Bill Pentak.* 7 secrets to managing productive people.
- **Fresh Wind Fresh Fire.** *By Jim Cymbala* What happens when God's Spirit invades the heart of His people?
- **Love, Acceptance and Forgiveness.** *By Jerry Cook & Stanley C. Baldwin* Being a Christian in a non-Christain world.
- **Emotionally Healthy Spirituality.** *By Peter Scazzero* It's impossible to be spiritually mature while remaining emotionally immature.
- **Emotionally Healthy church.** *By Peter Scazzero* A strategy for discipleship that actually changes lives.
- **Fathered by God.** *By John Eldridge* Being Fathered by God.
- **A Praying Life.** *By Paul E. Miller* Connecting with God in a distracting world.
- **Keep Your Love On.** *By Danny Silk* Connection, Communication and Boundaries.
- **The Bondage Breaker.** *By Neil T. Anderson.* Overcoming negative thoughts, irrational feelings and habitual sin.

One of the other great resources we have is our life. Learn from your mistakes. Every challenge is an opportunity to become more aware and emotionally intelligent, so don't waste a single experience good or bad and be a life learner who is willing to embrace change.

LETS GO A BETTER WAY

My final encouragement is simply to welcome you to the Better Way journey. Trust me when I say you have made the best decision and will not regret a single moment. The Better Way life is going to transform you from the inside out and you will never be the same.

As we come to the end of this book, I would like to finish with a prayer for you, because there is no doubt in my mind God has placed my story in your hand and has a great plan for you.

> *Father,*
> *I pray for those who are holding this book right now.*
> *I ask you to give them fresh eyes to see and new ears to hear what you are saying.*
> *Help them, like you have helped me, to embrace the change you want to bring in their lives.*
> *And help them to be strong and courageous as they face the giants before them.*
> *I thank you Lord, for you have given them everything they need to succeed and break the cycles holding them back.*
> *Renew their mind and bring freedom where there are strongholds.*
> *Give them faith when they doubt and grace when they stumble.*
> *May your goodness and faithfulness lead and guide them into a Better Way, a way in which emotional health and spiritual maturity meet.*
> *Amen!*

If you would like to start the Better Way Journey and want some support, or maybe you just want to share your story? Please feel free to contact me. I would love to hear from you.

A Better Way.
Email: letsgoabetterway@gmail.com

Dave.

www.ingramcontent.com/pod-product-compliance
Lightning Source LLC
Chambersburg PA
CBHW021328060726
47591CB00006B/1926